Garden
MADE

D0775046

Purchased from
Multnomah County Library
Title Wave Used Bookstore
216 NE Knott St, Portland, OR

Garden
MADE

A Year of Seasonal Projects
to Beautify Your Garden
and Your Life

STEPHANIE ROSE

Roost Books
BOSTON LONDON
2015

Roost Books
An imprint of Shambhala Publications, Inc.
Horticultural Hall
300 Massachusetts Avenue
Boston, Massachusetts 02115
roostbooks.com

Text and photographs © 2015 by Stephanie Rose
Photo of Sir the Squirrel, page 103, courtesy of
Melissa J. Will, http://empressofdirt.net/.
Photographs on pages x, 7, 47, 132, and 133
courtesy of Michael Rose.

The lists of night-flowering plants and night-fragrant
plants on pages 74–75 are adapted from *The Night
Shift* by Judy Sedbrook, Colorado State University
Cooperative Extension Master Gardener Program,
Denver County (www.colostate.edu/Depts/
CoopExt/4DMG/Flowers/night.htm). Reprinted
with permission by the Colorado State University-
Denver Extension Master Gardener Program.

All rights reserved. No part of this book may be re-
produced in any form or by any means, electronic
or mechanical, including photocopying, recording,
or by any information storage and retrieval system,
without permission in writing from the publisher.

9 8 7 6 5 4 3 2 1

First Edition
Printed in the United States of America

♾This edition is printed on acid-free paper that
meets the American National Standards Institute
Z39.48 Standard.
♻ Shambhala makes every effort to print on
recycled paper. For more information please visit
www.shambhala.com.

Distributed in the United States by Penguin Random House LLC and in Canada by Random House
of Canada Ltd

BOOK DESIGN BY SHUBHANI SARKAR

Library of Congress Cataloging-in-Publication Data

Whitney-Rose, Stephanie.
Garden made: a year of seasonal projects to
beautify your garden and your life/Stephanie Rose.
—First edition.
pages   cm
ISBN 978-1-61180-174-3 (pbk.: alk. paper)
1. Color in gardening. 2. Gardening. I. Title.
SB454.3.C64W45 2015
635—dc23
2014036762

Asher,

you are the best thing I have ever made.

———————

Michael,

I couldn't have done it without you.

1. SPRING

2. SUMMER

CONTENTS

3. FALL

4. WINTER

  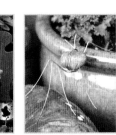

a garden *is*, and what we want of our gardens today. Miss Fairbrother has an interesting mind and an adroit pen, and the journey her readers take through the Dark Ages and their monastic gardens, the Middle Ages and their romantic ones through Tudor England, and the formal ja... and his followers, in both E... and eighteen-century England, is ... her as a guide.

... Buckner Hollingsworth, *Her Garden* ... Macmillan ... promising ... to break new ground by ... little known women gardeners, botanists, bot... ...ors, and garden writers who have played ... ...al history of this country. The author's m... ... of Geoffrey Taylor's, but whereas Dr. Ta... ...e Victorian era ... and devotes more ... ...h portrai... ...hemoirs of just four ... ...n his fi... ...ns, William Robinson, th... ...r-den rev... ...ald Farrer, the gifted and ec-centric plant... ...s. Hollingsworth covers the field fro... ...ys to the very near past, and gives ... ...graphical sketches of women whose ... ...07 to 1863. The brevity is not the ... ...lot of research has gone into this ... ...with pleasant and surprising results, but when I had finished reading it I had the slightly uneasy feeling that in the early biographies there had been too little source ... ...th ...sh out the bare bones of fact, and that the

PREFACE

IT WASN'T UNTIL ADULTHOOD THAT I TOOK TO GARDENING.
I grew up a city girl through and through, with little interest or knowledge
about where our food came from or how plants grew. Most of my life had
been spent in artificially lit offices or classrooms. I was a typical "brown
thumb" who believed I just didn't have the touch to nurture a plant. Then
one day I got sick. I mean, *I-could-not-get-out-of-bed-for-a-year* sick. When
the fog started to clear and I needed to rebuild my body, mind, and life from
the very beginning, I found a ray of hope outside my front door. I decided
to try gardening to help break up the long, monotonous days of recovery.

Off I went to the library to borrow more than a few books on gardening.
I read them while I lay in bed recovering from the library trip. I toured the
sparse and neglected plants on my property. There was mostly grass, but
also a few trees and shrubs, some that even flowered. I went to a hardware
store and bought some tools. I snipped here and weeded there, and it felt
pretty good, even if I was getting out for only an hour each week. Eventually I had weeded and snipped so much that there was bare soil. I went to
a garden center and bought a few flowers. More library books, more tools,
more plants, more recovery. I spent my time in bed reading about botany
and worked up the energy to get out and practice what I was learning. Day
by day I got stronger. I'd fall back into bed achy, exhausted, and gleefully
happy. Things were changing, I was getting better, life looked more hopeful.

Over the years, I looked for ways to garden every day and continue my
healing journey. With energy more limited than ambition, I started with
small, achievable projects that I knew I could complete. Instead of growing
fruit trees, which take many years to produce, I grew tomatoes in pots that
I could eat in a few months. With every success or failure from a smaller
project I was able to develop a base of knowledge and grow my confidence.
Eventually I did grow fruit trees—espaliered, multivariety trees at that—
and although those first apples were hard to wait for, I am more seasoned
and patient. Nurturing a tree for five years before I can eat an apple no
longer feels like more work than reward, because I can take on riskier projects as a more experienced gardener. Plus, it is now the act of caring for the
tree that feeds me, even if it was the promise of fruit that originally got me
hooked.

From that first spark the desire to connect with the earth came from
somewhere deep within. Now I could not imagine my life without it. I take

pleasure in the fresh air, dirty fingernails, striking plants, and delicious food while I work out the creaks from my bones and the frustrations from my mind. It's not that gardening is a magical cure-all that will fix whatever ails me, but a few hours spent with my troubles on the back burner and some muck on my boots can make a huge difference in the day.

I am now a Master Gardener in Vancouver, where I volunteer my time to teach school children and adults about organic gardening, growing food, and craft projects for the garden. I create, write, and photograph gardening and crafts as a freelance writer and on my blog, *Garden Therapy* (http://gardentherapy.ca). I grow ornamental plants to beautify my garden tucked in with vegetables and herbs to feed me. I've discovered a childlike passion for learning how food is grown, starting seeds, canning jam, and arranging cut flowers, all while rebuilding my body and soul. I'm not recovered yet—I may never be fully—but I was able to become well enough to expand my family, adding a bouncing baby boy to the mix all while creating the projects for this book. These are dreams I never could have even imagined all those years ago. I'm happy to have the opportunity to share a sneak peek into my world of garden therapy through each of the chapters. I hope it brings you as much joy and healing as it has for me.

Garden
MADE

INTRODUCTION

"YOU *MADE* THAT?"

This is possibly the question I get asked most often as I go about my life of gardening and crafting. It shouldn't be a surprise that most of what is found around my home and garden has been made by my two hands. On the one hand, I'm a gardener, learning the science of horticulture as each year presents new challenges and experiments in my outdoor space. On the other hand, I'm a maker, crafting everything from my own soaps to jams, home decor to light fixtures. As I spend time creating the right environment for plants to thrive, the crafter in me fills the space with functional art. As I craft handmade gifts and home and yard decor, I use the natural elements found in the garden as materials.

Garden Made showcases a year of these projects, made by hand and finished with finesse, ready to adorn your space or give as a gift. There are more than forty projects on these pages that I hope will inspire you, no matter what the season. Yes, even winter. *Garden Made* is a year-long journey of crafting and gardening that does not need to break for the weather. The themes differ by the natural cycle of the garden, but the joy of garden making need not be limited to one or two fair seasons a year. This book is divided into four chapters, one for each season— spring, summer, fall, and winter—so you need only to flip open the pages and find the project that gets you excited to start making.

"How on earth do you find the *time?*"

Ah, the second most common question I get asked. The answer is simple: I don't craft and garden because I *have* to, I do it because I *want* to. I make the time because it is time well spent. A bit of time in the garden relieves stress and works out those cricks and creaks. A few moments stolen to craft is a lot cheaper than therapy when I've got the blues. Working through a project is a harmonious experience that reboots my system into a state of quiet joy.

When I write "project," please do not be afraid. These are short bursts of bliss that can be fit into a limited schedule, completed quickly, and then enjoyed for months and years to come. Forget about backbreaking labor, complicated plantings, or the horror of weeding. By pulling on a pair of garden gloves you can pack away what troubles you for a few hours. The projects in this book are designed so you can parcel off a bit of garden making into an afternoon or weekend and experience pure enjoyment. They are meant to

sweep you away, allow you to dive in to a sensory experience that engages your body and mind, and leave you with something beautiful to enjoy in your home or garden.

No matter what your level of experience, the ideas in *Garden Made* are intended to inspire you with delightful imagery but not be so complex they can't be easily duplicated. The materials have been carefully selected to be accessible, and in cases where there is special equipment required, you can find resources at the end of this book to help you locate them. There are gardening tips and plant lists throughout the pages, set alongside a wide variety of crafting techniques that are simple but fun to try, such as paper-making, wood burning, and needle felting.

Whether you are a newbie gardener with a few pots on the fire escape, a lifelong gardener with acreage to tend, or somewhere in between, *Garden Made* was written for you to enjoy yourself in the garden. Lives are busy and days are filled with demands, but I hope this book encourages you to carve out a little time to connect with beauty and nature, revitalizing a weary body and calming a racing mind. I wish for you to feel the healing benefits of a little time crafting with plants and how it can change perspectives, bring new energy, and inspire pride in your accomplishment. Please join me on a journey of garden making. I'd love for the artful creations that surround your space to make you smile when you walk by, remembering the joy of a little time in the garden and the satisfaction of making something by hand.

You made that.

1

SPRING

HELLO, SPRING.

The ground thaws and shoots emerge through the soil. The air may still be chilly and what's left in the garden looks a bit rough around the edges, but I take pause for a moment to observe the mess and notice a few bulbs emerging, new growth hiding in the brown branches, leaf buds on the trees. Can you feel what's happening below the surface in your garden? There is a symphony of life just waiting to rush forth. All the energy stored up over a restful winter's sleep can hardly be contained by fallen leaves and bits of earth. It's the beginning of the gardening year. The plants are ready. Grab some muck boots and a rain jacket. The time is finally here!

Spring is my favorite time of the year for working in the garden. It's a chance to plan and create, to build the foundation for the year. Gardening can be cold and wet and muddy, but the rosy glow it puts on my cheeks is testament to how good it feels to shake off the cobwebs and dig in again. Growth is slow at first, but before long flowers will fill up the beds and (lettuce) leaves will fill up my plate. Projects this season will find you marking your ground with twig garden markers, labeling herbs with metal-stamped plant tags, and even recycling soda cans into herb labels for a "garnish garden." Planting herbs inside on a sunny windowsill will start the season early and they provide plenty of inspiration to liven up family meals.

The flora is exerting great effort to grow and prosper, and work tirelessly all year to produce beauty and nourishment for my family. The spring garden inspires me to show appreciation to those who also work tirelessly for others: mothers, teachers, friends. I'm eager to get into the garden and make something by hand for those I love. Crafty projects like painted mason jars, homemade seed paper, and a tea garden are child-friendly projects that make thoughtful handmade presents.

When the rain dries up in late spring, I burst through the door to get the first sunny-day projects started. The rhubarb needs harvesting: the tart stalks are destined for pie and the giant, ruffled leaves become the form for a birdbath. Birds are such an essential part of a garden that it's wise to welcome them. In my garden you will find busy birds plucking lengths of colorful yarn from a treetop box I've set out as a "bird nest helper." It's entertaining to watch our avian friends flit around with colorful pieces of yarn in their beaks, turning early morning coffee into dinner theater.

Shall we begin our journey of garden making? The projects you will find in this chapter are simple and family-friendly, allowing us to ease into the gardening year with kindness, craftiness, and merriment.

GARNISH GARDEN

with

SODA-CAN HERB LABELS

EVERY DAY I COOK WITH AT LEAST

some ingredients from the garden—herbs being a staple. No matter what the season, I zip down the back stairs to the herb garden, where perennial herbs like rosemary, sage, oregano, anise, mint, chamomile, and chives thrive. When springtime arrives, I tuck in annual herbs like parsley, tarragon, and basil. What results is a lush, fragrant garden that produces far more than I can use.

These outdoor herbs are a wonderful resource, but when I slave over a culinary delight, I like to garnish the dish with only the most pristine leaves. Growing herbs indoors guarantees that you'll have leaves that look as pretty as they taste. Choose herbs that complement what you normally cook and change it up each season. My year-round favorites are sage, parsley, chives, mint, and something sweet like anise or pineapple sage.

Make your garnish garden stand out even more with some handmade labels. These metal herb labels take recycling to a whole new level; you would never guess that they were made from soda cans! The elegant finish is contrary to the simplicity with which they are made. An ordinary ballpoint pen, used to add lettering (in your own handwriting or by tracing script from a computer printout), will add a uniquely personal touch to labels or gift tags.

MATERIALS

FOR THE GARNISH GARDEN
Indoor garden pots with tray
Coffee filters
Indoor potting soil
Potted herbs: parsley, chives, sage

FOR THE SODA-CAN HERB LABELS
Soda can
Craft punch (optional; see Resources)
Scissors
Single-hole punch
Computer, printer, paper (optional)
Ballpoint pen
Black permanent marker
Sponge with scrubber backing
Twine

Planting the Garden

Plant your garnish garden in a set of plant pots that will fit on a window-sill or an area near sunlight. Look for pots that have drainage holes but also a drip tray to protect the window ledge or furniture. Line each of the pots with a coffee filter to prevent the soil from washing out of the drainage holes. Plant the herbs in each pot with enough room for the roots to grow. Use a little indoor potting soil to fill in the space around the roots and water thoroughly.

1

Soda-Can Herb Labels

To make soda-can herb labels: for each plant, cut the top and bottom off a soda can and then cut down one side, to create a long rectangle of aluminum. (SEE PHOTOS: 1, 2.)

Cut out the shape of your tag, or use a heavy-duty craft punch to create uniform shapes. Use a single-hole punch to create a hole on both sides of the tag. As the aluminum will curl back into the shape of a can, punch single holes on the ends that bend in. When tied to the pot, the tag will lie flat. (SEE PHOTO: 3.)

2

Use a ballpoint pen to emboss words for your labels onto the aluminum. Or if you'd prefer, pick a font on the computer and print out the words for your labels, then use a ballpoint pen to trace the font onto the tag. Trace the embossed lettering with a permanent marker; then use the scrubby side of a damp kitchen sponge to buff off the marker, leaving behind black ink in the lines made by the ballpoint pen. This will help the lettering to stand out. (SEE PHOTO: 4.)

3

To tie the labels onto the plant pots, loop one-quarter of a length of twine through one end of the label, wrap both the long and short ends around the back of the pot, and loop the long end of the twine through the opposite hole on the label. Take the two short lengths of twine and tie them at the back of the pot. (SEE PHOTOS: 5, 6, 7.)

4

5

6

7

A garnish garden is a lively addition to kitchen decor but also a foodie's delight. Long gone are the days when a parsley stem is tossed on the side of a plate to adorn it. Today, garnishes are meant to be consumed. They add flavor and color, and in many cases they raise the dish to a new level of culinary pleasure.

Crispy Sage

If you think potato chips are addictive, wait until you try crispy sage. Fry sage by heating one tablespoon of olive oil and a dab of butter in a pan. When the butter melts, swish the pan liquids together. When the oil is good and hot, add a few fresh sage leaves. Flip sage leaves to fry evenly on both sides. The leaves will fry quickly, needing only five or ten seconds per side. Set them to cool on a paper towel to absorb extra oil. Top savory dishes with a fried sage leaf, which goes especially well with pork.

Parsley Salad Dressing

Salad dressing made with an abundance of fresh parsley is an old Italian recipe that tastes unbelievably rich and creamy. To make, add a handful of clean, fresh parsley to a food processor with one clove of garlic, one-quarter cup of extra-virgin olive oil, and one-quarter cup white balsamic vinegar. Blend until smooth. Add salt and pepper to taste. This recipe takes only moments to make, which is a good thing because the parsley dressing is best when used fresh.

Chive Oil

Chives are a pretty addition to the garden with their purple pom-pom flowers, but they also have just enough oniony oomph to elevate an ordinary dish. A creamy butternut squash soup becomes a restaurant-worthy dish when topped with chive oil and garlic croutons. Whip up chive oil by pureeing two large handfuls of chives and a cup of olive oil in a blender. Transfer to a pot and heat for a few minutes. Strain through a sieve lined with a coffee filter and chill. Chive oil lasts well in the fridge for up to one week.

HOMEMADE SEED PAPER

SEED PAPER IS A BEAUTIFUL AND

thoughtful way to share gardening with your friends and family. Whether it is used to make cards, gift tags, or other crafts, it is a sentiment that is most appreciated when torn up and buried in the earth!

Seed paper is made by using traditional papermaking techniques, during which seeds are embedded. Use handmade seed paper as you would any other craft paper: to make cards, gift tags, wrapping paper, bookmarks, envelopes, bows, or flowers. This disposable gift doesn't just get tossed in the garbage after it has served its decorative purpose; instead it gets planted and begins a new life as flowers, vegetables, or herbs. The garden that seed paper grows will be enjoyed year after year, creating beauty and nourishing those who receive it.

MATERIALS

Two artist canvases, with wood frames at least 1" thick

Window screen

Scissors

Utility knife

Staple gun

Shredded paper (see Note)

Blender (an old blender or a dedicated craft blender is best)

Plastic tub large enough to comfortably fit the frames inside

Sponge

Seeds

Decorative items (optional; see Note)

Towel

Nonstick surface (such as granite, glass, Plexiglass, or silicone)

NOTE: What paper makes the best paper? Try using these items: shredded bills and junk mail; gift wrap and tissue paper; printer paper, magazines, and newspapers; toilet tissue, paper towels, and napkins; paper bags and nonwaxed cardboard packaging; card stock and construction paper.

INSTRUCTIONS

To make paper with a uniform thickness and size, you first need to make a papermaking mold and deckle. Remove the canvas from both of the artist canvases, leaving two wooden frames. Cut the window screen so that it is larger than the wood frame, wrap it around the edges of one of the frames, and staple in place. Pull the screen quite taut around the frame while stapling. You will end up with one frame with a firm screen across the front (mold) and another wood frame of the same size (deckle). With the mold on the bottom (screen mesh side up) and the deckle on top, you have made your very own papermaking screen. (SEE PHOTOS: 1, 2, 3.)

Grab a handful of shredded paper including some colorful bits of tissue paper, craft paper, wrapping paper, or whatever paper you can find with some dye in it. Add the paper to the blender so that it is one-half to two-thirds full when gently compacted. Fill the blender to the fill line with warm water and let it sit for an hour or until the paper breaks apart easily when touched. A thicker-weight paper will take longer to soften than tissue paper.

When the paper is thoroughly softened, whir it in the blender until you have a thick, pulpy slurry. (SEE PHOTOS: 4, 5, 6.)

Fill the plastic tub with enough warm water to allow the mold and deckle to be submerged. Now float the papermaking screen in the water, deckle side up. (SEE PHOTO: 7.)

While holding the mold and deckle together, pour the slurry onto the screen. (SEE PHOTO: 8.)

Swish and wiggle the mold in the water to level the slurry and achieve about a one-quarter-inch thickness. Keep the top frame of the deckle out of the water so the slurry doesn't spill into the tub.

Now is the time to add your seeds and decorative elements. Sprinkle seeds on the level slurry, gently press them in, and cover them up with some of the pulp. If you accidentally create a hole in the paper, wiggle it in the water to once again create a uniform thickness. Be creative in decorating your paper. The best items to use are flat and light such as flower petals, leaves, or grasses; seed catalogs and magazines (torn into smaller pieces); foil or glittery wrapping paper (torn into smaller pieces); waxed paper products like milk cartons and coffee cups; string or yarn; dryer lint. (SEE PHOTOS: 9, 10, 11.)

Hold both sides of the frame and slowly lift it from the water, allowing excess water to drain. Remove the deckle, turn the screen over, and press (paper side down) onto a smooth nonstick surface. Sponge away the moisture by pressing down on the back of the screen and squeezing the sponge out into the tub. (SEE PHOTOS: 12, 13.)

Repeat until not much moisture remains on the sponge. Gently remove the screen, leaving the paper on the nonstick surface. (SEE PHOTO: 14.)

1

2

3

4

8

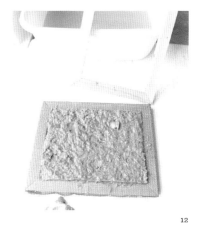

12

5

9

13

6

10

14

7

11

Gently shape and clean up the edges with the sponge, then set the paper aside somewhere that it will be undisturbed while drying, which could take up to a few days.

When the paper has dried, the edges may have curled. To flatten, simply stack all the dry sheets under a heavy pile of books and leave for a few days.

MAKING PAPER ROSES

To make these cheerful paper roses, cut the paper into a circle. Cut a spiral into the circle without cutting through to the end. Begin the spiral with a fairly thin width (about a quarter of an inch) and gradually get thicker. Don't worry if the cuts aren't uniform; a varying thickness along the spiral will just add to the organic appearance of the petals. Leave a 1½-inch-diameter circle in the center of the spiral.

Roll the spiral around itself starting at the outside edge continuing all the way to the center.

Add a few dabs of nontoxic glue where needed to hold the rose petals in place.

PLANTING INSTRUCTIONS

If you have made paper roses, they can be planted directly in the soil as is. For larger sheets of paper, tear them into half-inch pieces and scatter them on moist soil. Cover with a thin layer of soil and water. Keep moist until the seedlings emerge, then care for them as instructed on the seed packet. Seed paper can be grown in pots or directly in the garden. The instructions on the seed packet will be the same for seed paper, although for some types of seeds germination rates may be lower. Generally the seeds are placed in the wet paper pulp briefly, so this shouldn't damage the seed as long as the paper is stored in a dry location and used within a relatively short period of time. Germination rates decline as seeds age so it's best to use them within the year they were purchased.

TWIG GARDEN MARKERS

FLOWERS THAT GROW FROM BULBS

are such a pleasant treat in the spring. I tend to tuck bulbs in my garden beds between perennials to fill in the garden and extend bloom time. When the spring arrives and the perennials are still spreading out within their designated spaces, the gaps in between become the showstoppers of the garden by producing clusters of bright and cheery tulips, crocuses, snowdrops, daffodils, and grape hyacinths, many of which bloom much earlier than the perennials.

After carefully choosing bulbs in the fall, laying out a design, and giving the garden bed a nice, warm layer of mulch for the winter, inevitably I will thrust that overeager spade right through the bulbs as soon as the soil thaws. Don't get me wrong, I want to see my bulbs bloom, I really do. I may have even made some effort to note it on a garden plan, warning me of these potential land mines. Once spring garden fever hits, however, I cannot be trusted to slow down for a minute to save those bulbs. Full of digging fervor, nothing short of a neon sign that reads BULBS HERE with arrows pointing to the soil will stop me.

Perhaps the need for a blinking sign is an exaggeration. A homemade garden marker will do just fine in a pinch. Plus, if it's going to adorn my garden all year, then it should look natural and attractive as well as have some staying power. For these reasons sturdy twigs are more than suitable as bulb markers for unrelenting gardeners.

MATERIALS

Straight branch cuttings

Bypass pruners

Vegetable peeler

Wood-burning tool set

(see Resources)

INSTRUCTIONS

Hunt for branches anywhere from one-quarter to one inch thick and six inches long that are straight lengths and solid wood all the way through. (SEE PHOTO: 1.)

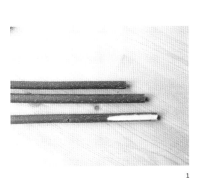

1

Use a vegetable peeler to carve a flat area at the top of the twig. (SEE PHOTO: 2.)

Use the wood-burning tool to burn the name of the bulbs onto the twig. Add decorative elements like hearts, which could also be read as arrows ("bulbs here!"). (SEE PHOTOS: 3, 4.)

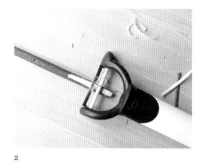

2

3

4

METAL-STAMPED
PLANT TAGS

THE AISLES OF A HARDWARE STORE

showcase a cornucopia of weird and wonderful things that can be repurposed for use in the garden. A metal alphabet stamp kit is one of my favorite hardware finds. I can hammer out some frustrations and feed the need to organize my plants all at once. Metal washers make for permanent plant tags that appeal to a modern aesthetic.

1

MATERIALS

Black permanent marker

Washers

Earplugs

Steel block (see Resources)

⅛" metal stamp set
   (see Resources)

Hammer

Steel wool

14-gauge galvanized wire

Wire cutters

Needle-nose pliers

Twine

INSTRUCTIONS

Set the washer on the steel block. Use a permanent marker to mark the letter placement with small dots on the metal washer. Position the letters along the bottom edge of the washer (that is, the part closest to you) to ensure they read upright when hanging. (SEE PHOTO: 1.)

Don your earplugs (hearing safety first!) then choose a letter stamp and position it on the first dot. Hammer hard without moving the letter out of position for about ten strikes.

When the label is complete, color in the newly stamped letter with the marker and then scuff off the excess with steel wool; this will darken the letter and help it to stand out. (SEE PHOTOS: 2, 3.)

Make a stake of metal wire for ground plants by cutting a length of wire six inches longer than you want it to stand above the soil. Bend the bottom of the wire with the needle-nose pliers into a V shape; this will create stability in the soil. Curl the top of the wire around the washer into a decorative curlicue, again using the needle-nose pliers. (SEE PHOTOS: 4, 5, 6, 7, 8.)

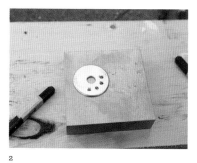

3

3

4

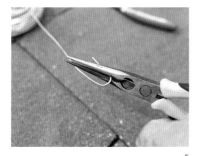

5

6

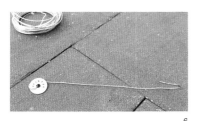

7

8

9

Alternatively, use garden twine to hang metal-stamped plant labels from tree branches to mark the variety of a fruit tree. This becomes especially handy when growing grafted trees with different varieties of fruit on different branches. (SEE PHOTO: 9.)

RUSTIC GARDEN SIGN

FREE RANGE escargot

A WEATHERED SIGN CAN BE A

welcoming sight in the garden. Whether it's for claiming ownership (STEPHANIE'S GARDEN), offering a practical suggestion (RING BELL. IF NO ANSWER, PULL WEEDS), or just plain fun (I DON'T REMEMBER PLANTING THIS), a sign personalizes the space for all to see. A salvaged piece of barn board or a weathered scrap of wood often makes the best backdrop, but it's not always easy to find reclaimed materials. I snap up aged wood when I find it, but a new cedar fence board will do just fine if nothing older is available.

MATERIALS

Cedar fence board or scrap wood
    cut to size

Wood stain in a bright color
    (such as blue or green)

Foam brush

Rag

Outdoor latex paint in two colors:
    one in a neutral color (such as
    putty or gray) and one in white
    or pastel (such as pale blue)

Paintbrushes

Coarse-grit sandpaper
    (such as 60 grit)

Craft paint

Stencils or stamps (optional)

Acrylic sealer (see Resources)

Hanging hardware

INSTRUCTIONS

Use a scrap of wood that is cut to the shape you would like for your sign. Rough edges, cracks, and knots only add to the rustic nature of the final look.

Stain the wood with a bright color, like blue or green. Apply stain with a foam brush, then wipe off with a clean rag. (SEE PHOTOS: 1, 2.)

When the stain is dry, mix four parts of a neutral-color, outdoor latex paint to one part water. Mix well. Brush the paint on in quick strokes, partially covering the stain. Allow it to dry then repeat, mixing a second color of paint, such as white or a pale pastel, with water and brushing it on the board. (SEE PHOTO: 3.)

Once the paint is dry, use a coarse-grit sandpaper to sand the board

3

2

1

and reveal the wood grain, then wipe clean. The board is now ready to be decorated. (SEE PHOTOS: 4, 5.)

Use craft paint, stencils, or stamps to create your message. The lettering on the escargot sign in the photos was painted freehand and outlined in permanent marker. "Free Range" was printed from the computer and then traced over transfer paper onto the sign before being painted with acrylic craft paints. (SEE PHOTO: 6.)

Sand the finished lettering to rough it up and give it an aged look. Wipe clean and spray an acrylic sealer on the wood to protect it from the elements. Add hanging hardware and mount your sign for all to see. (SEE PHOTOS: 7, 8.)

4

5

6

7

8

Looking for inspiration to add personality to your garden? Here are some ideas to help you pick the perfect prose:

Gardening is cheaper than therapy, and you get tomatoes.
So many weeds, so little thyme.
The grass is greener where you water.
Dig in!
Ring bell. If no answer, pull weeds.
Life is better in the garden.
Weeds for sale. U-Pick.
I don't remember planting this.
Grow, dang it!
Weed It and Reap
Backyard Paradise
GROW
BLOOM
May all your weeds be wildflowers.
Talk Dirt to Me
Gardeners Know All the Dirt
Sow Ready for Spring
It's spring. I'm so excited I wet my plants!
There's No Place Like Garden
There's Gnome Place Like Home
Gardening Makes the Heart Bloom
Never Enough Thyme
Trespassers Will Be Composted
Now Entering the Seedy Part of Town
I Dig Gardening
Keep Calm and Garden On

PAINTED MASON JAR
TULIP VASES

AS A GARDENER, ONE OF THE MOST

useful vases I've found is the simple mason jar. With this discovery, long gone are the mismatched vases that don't store easily but are needed for different types of arrangements. Now when I have an arrangement freshly snipped from the garden, I simply find a jar that fits and display it proudly. Large jars work well for long stems and smaller jars for short stems or floating blooms. Regular-mouth jars will contain a looser arrangement while wide-mouth jars can be packed full.

Painting jars allows for the vintage features to shine or simply transforms a contemporary canning jar. Add a flower frog lid and you have the ideal vessel for spring's favorite flowers: tulips.

MATERIALS

FOR THE JAR

Vintage or decorative wide-mouth
mason jars
Outdoor latex paint with primer
combination in white (see Note)
Latex craft paint in deep turquoise
(or other color choice)
Foam brush
Sandpaper (80 grit)
High-gloss aerosol sealer
(see Resources)

FOR THE FLOWER FROG LID

Mason jar ring and snap lid
High-gloss spray paint specifically
for metal
Permanent marker
Hardware mesh fencing (¼" squares)
Wire cutters

NOTE: Choosing paint is the most important step in this project. The goal is to get an opaque finish that is durable and water resistant. Many available glass paints result in a translucent, stained-glass look. Acrylic craft paints are wonderful for a lot of projects, but in this case they will peel off with just a little water dribbling down the side of the jar, even with a few solid layers of sealer on top.

The best choice for durability is an opaque spray paint made to adhere to glass. While it is simple to apply, the color choices are limited. To customize color or make many jars in different colors economically, use craft paint to tint a white outdoor latex paint-primer combination. For this project I used a deep turquoise craft paint mixed with white paint and primer. The result was a robin's egg blue that is a fitting shade for spring.

INSTRUCTIONS

To prepare the jar, mix craft paint and outdoor paint thoroughly and apply evenly to the outside of the jar with a foam brush. This could take three coats to get proper coverage. Allow the paint to dry between coats. (SEE PHOTO: 1.)

When you are happy with the opaqueness, use sandpaper to distress the finish. Sand away the paint on any raised surfaces to highlight the label, and scuff up a few spots around the jar as well. Wipe clean and spray with a high-gloss sealer.

After the sealer is completely dry, the vase is ready to use. As the inside is unfinished, it's fine to fill with water. The outside is protected from drips and can be cleaned by wiping it down. Don't submerge the vase in water or put in the dishwasher to avoid paint flaking off.

To prepare the lid, coat the mason jar ring lightly with spray paint. Use a light dusting of paint on a rusty gold ring for an antiqued look. Be sure to choose a spray paint that works with metal and has a high-gloss finish.

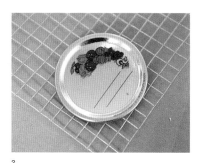

Using the snap lid as a template for the wire insert, mark the wire around the lid with permanent marker and snip it with wire cutters. The wire insert should be slightly larger than the inside of the ring so it will pressure-fit snugly in the ring. (SEE PHOTOS: 2, 3.)

Press the wire into the ring evenly until it is somewhat convex when on the jar. Screw the flower frog lid onto the painted jar. Add flowers that need some extra support, such as tulips. (SEE PHOTO: 4.)

BIRD NEST HELPERS

HAVE YOU EVER WATCHED BIRDS

feather their nests? They zoom in from all directions with a scrap of yarn, a clump of moss, or a piece of straw. Nesting birds prepare birdhouses and nests with a soft layer to protect and incubate their eggs, and cradle the hatchlings. If birds are building nests in your garden then you may very well find a few loose threads on any fabric left outdoors. A box of yarn and other material adds a colorful touch to the garden and our feathered friends' nests. Hang it somewhere near the nest or birdhouse, but also in a low-traffic area. If you can do so without disrupting the birds, locate the box somewhere your family can get prime viewing of the backyard happenings. It's a joy for kids of all ages to watch a little beak wrestle with some yarn before tucking it into the birdhouse.

MATERIALS

FOR THE BOX

¾-inch thick cedar
    (or other rot-resistant wood)
    cut as follows:
    Top: 4¾" × 12"
    Bottom: 4¾" × 12"
    Back panel: 5½" × 12"
    Left panel: 5½" square
    Right panel: 5½" square
Weather-resistant screws between
    1¼" and 1½" long (size #6 or #8)
Drill
Plastic bird netting
Staple gun

FOR THE NESTING MATERIALS

Scraps of yarn cut to 4"
Small fabric scraps
Wood shavings
Dryer lint
Pinecones
Straw or dried plant material
Hair (pet or human hair if you dare!)

1

2

3

Cut cedar boards to the dimensions listed using a table saw, or have the wood cut at your local hardware store.

Screw the box together by drilling pilot holes first as a guide, then using wood screws to secure the boards together. The top and bottom boards will screw into the side of the side boards, so lay out the pieces as they will be attached together. Hold one of the end pieces over a side piece where they are intended to attach and drill two pilot holes three-quarters of an inch from the edge. Screw the pieces together through the pilot holes. Add the other side piece and repeat the steps for making pilot holes and screwing the box together. Repeat steps for the other end of the box.

To attach the bottom of the box, set the bottom piece in place and drill four pilot holes, one on each side, and screw to secure. (SEE PHOTO: 1.)

Fill the box loosely with a variety of nesting materials. (SEE PHOTO: 2.)

Cut a section of netting two inches larger than the box. Use the staple gun to secure the netting on one side, then pull it tightly across the box and staple it in place on the other side. Repeat for the top and bottom.

Place the box in a tree or other sheltered location and get ready to watch the show! (SEE PHOTO: 3.)

I once heard a statistic on the number of aphids that a chickadee can eat. It was a big number—a *someone-get-me-a-chickadee-stat* kind of number, especially if you are fed up with aphids sucking the life from your garden. While I don't remember the exact number now, let me just say that having birds, any birds, in your garden is a good thing. They eat weevils, caterpillars, grubs, and a long list of other undesirable garden pests. Sure, they may pick at your strawberry patch or nibble at the blueberries. They will even take your precious earthworms early in the morning. But the benefits of birds do so far outweigh the drawbacks in many cases that it's nice to provide them with the things they need to move into your garden.

STRAWBERRIES in the SKY

STRAWBERRIES LOVE THE SUN AND

they are kind enough to not take up too much room in the soil—to produce a lot of berries—a fortunate quality, because you can sure eat plenty of sun-warmed strawberries while gardening. Gardeners aren't the only ones who love these super-sweet red treats; strawberries planted in the ground will be ripe for beetles, slugs, rodents, birds, and the dreaded strawberry-eating canine. No matter how well protected my berries are by netting, eggshells, or straw, inevitably I will be sharing them with the aforementioned critters. Even when I check the patch each day—watching as big berries start to turn color, anticipating the moment their juice will be dribbling down my chin—it seems the slugs and friends always get to them first. Tired of being outwitted by wildlife, I now like to grow strawberries in the sky. This vintage wire basket makes a fitting hanging container to keep the berries out of harm's way.

3

2

1

MATERIALS

Vintage wire basket

Moss

Container soil mix

Strawberry plant (for information about choosing, see "June-Bearing versus Ever-Bearing Varieties")

Chain basket hanger (see Resources)

INSTRUCTIONS

Line a basket with moss and fill it halfway with container mix soil. (SEE PHOTO: 1.)

Plant a strawberry plant and fill in some soil around the roots. (SEE PHOTO: 2.)

Add a chain basket hanger to suspend it in a sunny location. (SEE PHOTO: 3.)

As the planter is small and in direct sun, it will need regular watering, especially during fruiting. On hot days check moisture in both the morning and afternoon. You will be rewarded for your efforts in, well, strawberries. (SEE PHOTOS: 4, 5.)

4

5

JUNE-BEARING VERSUS EVER-BEARING VARIETIES

What is the difference between June-bearing and ever-bearing strawberries? If I were left to choose by just the names, I would certainly choose the "ever-bearing." Um, yeah, I want berries *all the time*, not just in June! However, the difference between these two types of berries is a bit more complex than that.

June-bearing strawberries are the first to ripen in the late spring or early summer. They will produce a lot of berries per plant, all within three weeks of the year. They are prolific spreaders that will send out a plethora of runners (aka baby strawberry plants) that you can use to fill in a large patch, plant elsewhere in the garden, or create more hanging baskets for.

Ever-bearing strawberries produce fewer berries at a time, but they continue to produce from summer until fall. They are less prolific in sending out runners, but they also maintain a nicer-looking ground cover or container plant.

For this hanging basket project, I chose a June-bearing variety and after the weeks of harvest were over, I moved the plants to the garden. Then I filled the planter with shade-loving annuals and hung it in a less sunny location, where I could still enjoy it but not have to worry about watering every day.

TEAPOT PLANTER

SOME PEOPLE MAY BE APPALLED BY

the found items I turn into planters. To spend forty dollars on a stunning vintage teapot that is "only" going to adorn the garden may be considered insanity to some. To a gardener—to me—it is with great respect that it earns a place outdoors. Coming home with me means this pot will be planted with fragrant mint and set in the garden to enjoy the days: to be a part of life and growth, to enjoy sounds and smells. The life of the pot may be shorter and less protected, but it will be more appreciated and will reflect the joy of being out in the garden.

This vintage silver teapot was planted with an apple mint and chocolate mint arrangement. Perched in a sunny window in spring, then into the garden for summer, it will grow and thrive until the leaves are picked to make tea.

MATERIALS

Vintage silver or pewter teapot
Safety goggles
Hammer and nail
Power drill with metal drill bit
Metal file

Container potting soil mix
Combination of mint plants such as
apple mint, ginger mint, chocolate mint, or peppermint

INSTRUCTIONS

First, decide where you are going to display your planter. If you plan to keep it indoors on a sunny windowsill, then you could skip the drainage holes at the bottom and be sure to not overwater the soil. (Planting in a teapot is pretty handy when you want to manage drainage. After watering, let the pot sit for five to ten minutes then pour off any excess through the spout.)

If you would like to leave your planter in the garden, add some drainage holes on the bottom to ensure that it doesn't get waterlogged by rain or sprinklers. For this step, you should protect your eyes with safety goggles. Hammer a nail where the drainage hole will go, in order to make a divot that will act as your guide for the drill. Use a power drill with a bit made specifically for metal and set the bit on the divot. Apply steady pressure to drill through the metal. Use a metal file to smooth out any burrs created from drilling. Please note: Metal gets very hot when drilling through it. Do not touch a freshly drilled hole or the bit until they have cooled.

Fill the bottom of the teapot with soil and plant the mint by adding a combination of different varieties.

HARVESTING MINT

Pick fresh mint leaves as you need them to use in recipes. Cutting or "pinching" the tops off the stems will promote bushier growth, as multiple side stems will grow from below the point where you cut as long as there are leaf nodes. Pinch at the height of the plant you want to fill out by looking for a slight bulge in the stem near the leaves: this is the node that will grow new stems, so pinch or cut directly above it. Harvest all the stems by cutting the whole plant to one inch from the soil just before the plant flowers.

Preserve mint leaves by drying them tied upside down in bunches. Hanging bunches in a warm, dark, well-ventilated environment is best. Store dried leaves in airtight containers to make tea throughout the year. Fresh mint leaves can also be frozen in freezer bags. Frozen leaves will quickly thaw when added to tea.

MINTY SUN TEA

Sun tea is a fun way to enjoy the freshness of summer. Using freshly harvested mint, herbs, or your favorite flavor of tea, let the sun do the work to brew the perfect cup. Fill a mason jar one-quarter of the way full with loosely packed mint leaves and top up with cool water. Cap the jar and leave in the sun for three to five hours. Strain and chill the tea, adding honey or sugar if you wish. If you choose to make sun tea from tea bags, add two to three bags per quart of water.

RHUBARB LEAF
for the BIRDS

———

THE FIRST TIME I TASTED A TART

rhubarb stalk dipped in sugar I was hooked! The flavor is surprisingly complex for a stem and when matched with something sweet it's a little slice of heaven. The leaves, on the other hand, are not so tasty (which is good, since they are toxic), but it's such a pity that this prolific plant hasn't more culinary uses. This project is my attempt to get a little more out of my rhubarb plants. The ruffled and very large leaves make a wonderful mold for a birdbath. Once cast in concrete, these rhubarb leaves will live on forever and supply garden birds with a watering hole.

MATERIALS

Large rhubarb leaf	Old trowel
Rubber gloves, protective glasses, and a mask	Plastic drop cloth
	Vegetable oil or cooking spray
Repair concrete (see Note)	Stiff bristle brush
Wheelbarrow or large bucket	Chisel and hammer (optional)
Water source (hose or watering can)	

NOTE: Choose a lightweight concrete mix (less gravel) for a smoother finished product; choose a heavier-weight concrete mix (more gravel) if the concrete will be in high traffic areas. The best product for small, decorative projects is a repair concrete, which has no large pieces of gravel in it.

INSTRUCTIONS

Begin by cutting a large rhubarb leaf off the stem, to use for your mold (see Harvesting Rhubarb on page 44 for instructions on how to harvest the stems). Choose a firm leaf with a strong shape. (If you can find any without holes then congratulations, you have won the slug war!) It's best to start this project at the beginning of the season when the leaves are strongest and less chewed. A few nibbles or holes are expected in an organic garden and won't take away from the final project.

Wearing protective gloves, glasses, and a mask, mix the concrete according to the manufacturer's instructions. While the measurements

5

6

7

and mixing instructions will be on the package, in general you will want a large container to mix a whole bag at once. An old wheelbarrow is ideal as the height makes mixing a bit easier. Add the concrete to the container first, then pour the recommended measure of water into the center. Stir thoroughly and use immediately. Consistency should be on the drier, firmer side. Add more dry mix if it is too runny. (SEE PHOTO: 1.)

Build a firm mound in the soil in the shape that you want your birdbath to take. Lay the plastic drop cloth over the mound and place the leaf, vein-side up, on the mound. Spray the back of the leaf thoroughly with cooking spray or brush with oil. (SEE PHOTOS: 2, 3, 4.)

Pile the concrete onto the leaf and pat it all around to compress the concrete and remove air bubbles. Spread the concrete to just half an inch from the edge of the leaf and gently round the extra half inch of leaf over the edge of the concrete. This will give the edges a more refined look. (SEE PHOTO: 5.)

Wrap the concrete in the plastic and allow it to dry for twelve hours if the outside temperature is hot and dry, or twenty-four hours if it is cooler and more humid. (SEE PHOTO: 6.)

Gently peel off the leaf before the concrete is set, being mindful that it can easily break or crack at this stage. Generally it would be preferable to wait until the concrete is completely dry to unmold it, but for this project you are trying to avoid the possibility of leaving too much plant material behind in the crevices. (SEE PHOTO: 7.)

Allow the concrete to cure completely according to the package instructions, then use a stiff bristle brush to scrub off any remaining plant material. You may also use a chisel and hammer to remove any concrete that has escaped the confines of the leaf, leaving a finished but still natural shape to the birdbath. (SEE PHOTO: 8.)

Set the birdbath upright in the garden, on a raised wood stump or atop some overturned clay pots. (SEE PHOTO: 9.)

8

9

Ensure your plant will continue to be fruitful by harvesting rhubarb the right way. Let a new plant grow for two years before harvesting any stalks and only take one-third of the plant on year three. After that you can harvest the plant pretty heavily, leaving the smaller stalks behind after a solid six to eight weeks of pulling off stems for pie and leaves for birdbaths.

To harvest the stems, solidly grasp the base of the stem, twist to the side, and pull to remove. Trim the leaves in a fan pattern for storing in the fridge or trim the tops completely if you plan to use the rhubarb right away. Whether stalks are red or green doesn't affect flavor, but the red stalks are generally preferred to make the cheery pink color often associated with rhubarb desserts.

2

SUMMER

THE GARDEN IS DOING ITS JOB IN THE

summertime. This is what it has been working all year for. This is what I have been working all year for. The garden has rested over winter, revved up mighty growth over spring, and now it's in bloom. Vivid petals gleam in colors that attract every pollinator in the vicinity, showing off the very best in the sizzling heat of the long days. Now is when gardens have their parade, their awards show, their pageant. The best and brightest flowers are displayed in bouquets. Yummy leaves, stems, and seedpods will be harvested and devoured; some plants will complete their life cycle and set fruit.

To me, gardening in summer consists of appreciating and celebrating the garden's flourishing beauty: Spending a morning touring the grounds and listening to the buzz of life that has been enjoying the space since the wee hours. Putting my feet up on a lounge chair to sip rhubarb lemonade. Enjoying the sweetly scented flora while puttering around in flip-flops, snacking on cherry tomatoes and crunching green beans.

Summer is the time to enjoy the fruits of your labor. Notice the inspiration that bursts around you in color, shapes, tastes, and aromas. Find time for projects that are more involved, ornamental, multifaceted; they are the showstoppers. Framed succulents hanging on outdoor walls will delight those who pass by. Floating plants dancing atop the pool of a fountain will add more life to an already lively flow of water. A wild-looking planter swinging from a vintage high chair whimsically hangs from a tree. Freshly harvested lavender tied to an old painting ladder perfumes the air.

Once the canvas is painted, the frames are hung, and the blooms are looking their best there is one thing left to do: gather.

Send out the invites. Light the candles. Invite children to explore under trees, pick sun-warmed fruit, and taste different herbs. Host friends and family for long meals on the patio and tours of the garden. Put your feet up and relax long into the warm night air.

A PICTURE GARDEN

THERE IS NOTHING TO SAY THAT

artwork must be contained to inside walls. Nor is there anything to say that it can't grow, morph, and change as the days go by. A picture garden is an accolade to the magical color and form created by Mother Nature herself. This project is ideal for small spaces or as a focal point in a larger one.

The beauty of living art is that it commands your focus. You must engage with it. While succulents are somewhat forgiving of neglect, drought, and vertical growing conditions, they still need your help to thrive.

Some living-art projects use succulent cuttings that require at least eight to twelve weeks to root and another few months for the teeny, tiny plants to fill in. Where weather is seasonal, that kind of schedule doesn't allow for much time to enjoy the finished project before it is necessary to overwinter the plants. This project has been designed so you can enjoy the finished piece after just four to six weeks.

MATERIALS

FOR THE FRAME

Plastic picture frame in any dimension you like as long as the frame itself is at least 2" wide (*Note:* These instructions are for a frame with an inner dimension of 10" × 12".)

Cedar board 1" × 3" × 6', for the box frame (*Note:* The actual dimensions of 1" × 3" milled lumber are ¾" × 2½".)

Wood screws as follows:

Four size #6 screws 1½" long

Four size #6 screws 1" long

Eight size #6 screws ½" long

Four ½" corner braces

One piece of ¼" hardware mesh fencing measuring 11¾" × 13¾"

One piece of ¼"-thick plywood measuring 12" × 14", for the bottom

Picture-hanging hardware

Tape measure and marker

Miter saw, circular saw, handsaw, or table saw

Drill and drill bits or screwdriver

Wire cutters

Staple gun

Pruning shears

Trowel

FOR THE PLANTING MATERIALS

Container soil mix (see "Container Soil Mix Recipe")

Mixed succulents in a variety of sizes (see Note)

NOTE: Purchase succulents potted in soil for this project. Certainly add cuttings if you have them, as different shapes, colors, and sizes will create the most interesting final project. For an economical solution, choose plants that have multiplied in their pots, with many pups (propagules or smaller plants growing from the succulent) that you can divide and spread throughout the frame. For this project, I purchased about ten four-inch pots of different succulents, which filled three frames. Pick plants in pristine condition; you want them to look their very best.

INSTRUCTIONS

Determine the size of the planter box based on the size of the picture frame. The inside dimensions of the planter box should be half an inch wider and half an inch longer than the inside dimensions of the picture frame. For this project, the inside dimensions of the box frame are 10½ inches wide by 12½ inches long.

Using a saw, cut the one-by-three-inch cedar board in four pieces for the sides of the planter box: two pieces 10½ inches long and two pieces 14 inches long. (SEE PHOTO: 1.)

Drill a pilot hole on either end of each 14-inch-long cedar board; center the holes on the short end of the board, three-eighths inch from the edge. Build the frame with the 10½-inch-long pieces between the two 14-inch-long pieces. Screw the boards together using the 1½-inch #6 screws. (SEE PHOTO: 2.)

Create mortises, or notches in the box frame, to receive the corner braces, so that the hardware will sit flush with the planter box when you use the braces to attach the picture frame. To make the mortises, center one of the corner braces along the top edge of one side of the planter box. With a marker, draw a line on either side of the corner brace. Do the same for the other three sides. (SEE PHOTO: 3.)

Within the marked lines, use a saw to cut out mortises to receive the corner braces. If you are using a table saw, set the saw blade height to the same height as the thickness of the corner brace, about an eighth of an inch. Run the box frame over the saw repeatedly within the marked lines of the corner brace. Repeat for each side until all four mortises are cut.

Place the corner braces in the mortises with the brace hanging over the inside of the box. Place the picture frame squarely on top of the box frame and mark the picture frame where the corner brace will be mounted. (SEE PHOTO: 4.)

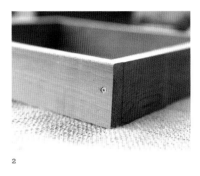

5

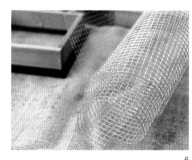

6

7

8

Attach the corner braces to the back of the picture frame using the half-inch #6 wood screws. Place the picture frame back on top of the box frame and ensure that the picture frame sits properly, with each corner brace fitting cleanly into its notch. Remove the frame and set it aside. (SEE PHOTO: 5.)

Using wire cutters, cut the hardware mesh to one-quarter inch smaller in both dimensions than the outside dimensions of the box frame: for this project the measurement will be 11¾ inches by 13¾ inches. Lay the hardware mesh on top of the box frame (with the corner brace notch side up) and with a staple gun attach the hardware mesh to the box frame. Using wire cutters, cut away the hardware mesh over the mortises. (SEE PHOTOS: 6, 7.)

Place the picture frame back on top of the box frame so the corner braces fit within the mortises, through the cut-out hardware mesh. Turn the box upside down, and using the other four half-inch #6 wood screws, attach the picture frame to the box frame through the corner braces.

Using a saw, cut the quarter-inch plywood to 12 by 14 inches, to match the outside dimensions of the box frame. Rest the plywood on the bottom of the box frame. Using a drill, center a pilot hole along one side of the plywood base three-eighths of an inch from the edge so that it aligns with the box frame. Do the same for the other three sides. Using a drill or screwdriver and the four one-inch #6 wood screws, attach the plywood base to the box frame.

Choose which way you will orient your frame, and mount your picture-hanging hardware. Ensure the hardware is rated for at least 15 pounds of hanging weight.

Planting and Care

Remove succulents from their pots and shake off some of the soil. Try to leave a little clump of soil just below the rosette so you have a root ball to plant. Pups can be removed from the mother plant by cutting them off at the base with clean pruning shears. Remove the lower leaves on each stem. You should have one or two inches of stem to stick in the soil to root.

Fill the box with container mix soil by scooping in the soil and shaking the box to settle it down. Water the box and leave for an hour for the soil to settle and compact. Top up with more soil and water again until it is quite full and the base of the soil is moderately firm (you should still be able to get your finger in the soil, but it will feel dense). (SEE PHOTO: 8.)

Lay out your design. Try planting larger rosettes in a *Z* or reverse *Z* pattern and fill in smaller succulents around them. Pick coordinating colors, or use all the colors; they are succulents, so they will naturally go together no matter what combination you choose! (SEE PHOTO: 9.)

Use wire cutters to snip holes in the hardware mesh that are just large enough for the mini root balls to fit in). Dig little holes in the soil and tuck the roots into them. Fill soil around the roots and gently press down to secure the plants in place. Continue making holes for the larger plants and add the cuttings to fill in your design. (SEE PHOTO: 10.)

Set the finished planter in a sunny location and water it. Keep the soil slightly damp for four to six weeks as everything roots into place. Gently tug the succulents to feel if the plants give resistance and are therefore rooted. Use this tug test to judge when the frame is ready to be mounted on the wall. (SEE PHOTO: 11.)

Hang the frame when the water has been absorbed by the soil enough that it doesn't drip out but the soil is still moist. After that, allow the soil to dry between watering, but not so much that the soil becomes hard and crusty. Frames placed in sunny, hot locations will dry out faster than those in shadier, cooler locations. (SEE PHOTO: 12.)

To water, take the frame down and lay it horizontally on a flat surface. Water slowly and allow the water to absorb into the soil for a few hours until you hang the frame back up again. (SEE PHOTOS: 13, 14.)

A frame filled with large, fast-growing succulents means that some care will be required at the beginning of the next season, when the succulents need refreshing, dividing, or trimming to put on a gorgeous show again.

9

10

11

12

13

14

Not all soil is the same. A trip to your local garden center will certainly show you a wide range of prices and ingredients. But it's all just dirt, right? Nope. The difference will be seen in the success of your plants. Soil is absolutely the most important ingredient of a healthy garden. Soil should be alive: full of good stuff like microbes, bacteria, and fungi. Garden soil should also be full of things like worms, beetles, and ants to aerate the soil, munch on bits of organic material, and leave behind nutrient-rich frass (bug poop) to feed your plants. If you are having problems with your garden, start with the soil. Dig in rich organic compost and stop using pesticides or herbicides. Keep the soil loose, dark, and healthy and your plants will thank you for it.

It's difficult to replicate the ecosystem of the garden in a container. Using garden soil in containers will make them heavy; garden soil will become compacted; and water will flow through too quickly. To combat these issues, buy a container soil mix or make your own with peat moss or coconut coir. Peat moss is a pH-balanced additive used to increase moisture content and prevent soil compaction. Coconut coir is a more eco-friendly alternative to peat moss. The recipe I often use is 40 percent peat moss or coconut coir and 60 percent high-quality organic soil. The soil you choose should be a rich, fully composted soil free from fertilizer or dyes.

FLOWER POUNDING

———

1

2

3

4

FLOWER POUNDING IS ESSENTIALLY

fabric printing: transferring the pigments in flowers and leaves onto fabric prepared to absorb and hold on to the color. It's a fun activity to do with kids who love the sound of rocks striking the board over and over and over and over.

There are two parts to flower pounding on fabric: preparing the fabric for pigment transfer, and bashing flowers with a rock. If you want to skip right to the bashing part, purchase pretreated fabric or use paper instead.

MATERIALS

100 percent cotton muslin	Long wooden spoon or stick
Laundry detergent	A collection of flowers and leaves
Washing soda (see Resources)	A rock or hammer
Alum (see Resources)	Wax or parchment paper
Bucket	A hard, flat, smooth surface
Rubber gloves	

INSTRUCTIONS

Fabric Preparation

If you will be preparing fabric yourself, first wash the muslin in a washing machine with regular laundry detergent and two tablespoons of washing soda. Run the rinse cycle two more times to ensure that the washing soda is removed.

In the bucket, dissolve two tablespoons of alum per quart of hot water. Wear rubber gloves to protect your hands, and use a long wooden spoon or stick to stir until the alum is dissolved, and then add the fabric. Allow the muslin to cool in the alum bath, then mix one teaspoon of washing soda into a half cup of water and add it to the bath (it will fizz and bubble right before your eyes!). Stir and let sit overnight.

In the morning, wring out the muslin (again using the rubber gloves) and dry in a dryer or by hanging. Iron when slightly damp to remove wrinkles.

Flower Pounding

Head out to the garden and search for flowers and leaves to print. Small, multipetaled flowers such as hydrangeas, calendulas, and violas work best, as it takes fewer strikes with a rock to print the complete shape. Gather a few large roses or Oriental poppies and give those a try as well; you can print parts of the larger petals and create free-form shapes. Fern leaves make wonderful prints, as do the colored leaves of a Japanese maple. There are many other leaves with shapes and color that could add to the design. Practice with different kinds of natural elements until you find a look that you like. (SEE PHOTO: 1.)

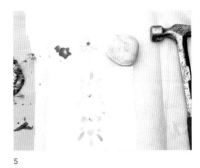

5

Lay out a piece of parchment on a hard, flat, smooth work surface. Cut a piece of the treated fabric and set your petal design on one half of it. When you are happy with your design, fold the fabric over to sandwich the petals between the two halves of fabric. Cover with another piece of parchment, and it's time to start pounding. (SEE PHOTOS: 2, 3.)

6

Hold the fabric firmly in place and start hitting the petals with the rock. You will quickly see the pigment transfer that is taking place. Continue until you have the amount of color that you like. Use different tools to create patterns. Try a hammer with a stippled head to make a polka-dot pattern on the petals. (SEE PHOTOS: 4, 5.)

When you are happy with your finished creation, set the dye by ironing the muslin on the highest setting for five minutes.

Use your new fabric art in sewing projects, for quilting, or in a frame as a wall hanging. (SEE PHOTO: 6.)

HARVESTING FLOWERS AND LEAVES FOR CRAFTS AND ARRANGEMENTS

While you may be in a hurry to gather a bouquet, ripping a bunch of flowers from the earth is not going to leave much for you to enjoy in the garden. Harvesting flowers for a craft project should be done using the same technique as cutting for a floral arrangement. Use clean, sharp scissors or pruners to clip the flower or leaf. Wash or wipe your pruners between plants to avoid spreading disease. Don't harvest more than one-third of an established plant, less (or not at all) for younger plants. Cut flowers early in the day and put them in water immediately to prevent wilting. By following these steps you will ensure that both the host plant and the cut blooms will continue looking their best.

A LIVING FOUNTAIN

WATER IN THE GARDEN IS A CALMING

and peaceful element. It allows birds, bugs, and bees to have a drink and keep cool on hot days. Even a small fountain can host a great number of annual water plants that propagate well through the season, look handsome, and are a whole lot of fun to grow!

MATERIALS

Fountain with a submersible pond pump

Floating aquatic plants (for help in choosing the plants for your fountain, see "Floating Aquatic Plants")

INSTRUCTIONS

Planting a living fountain is as simple as adding suitable aquatic plants to the water in the fountain. Visit a local garden center to see which plants are for sale in your area, then choose plants that suit the size and location (sun, shade, partial sun, or partial shade) of the fountain. Floaters, as you can imagine, are plants that grow, and thus float, on top of water. They are generally considered "ground covers" for ponds, providing background to more decorative water lilies, grasses, and ornamentals. For small spaces and ease of care, floaters are a good choice for creating a living fountain and can certainly stand alone in a decorative water feature.

Caring for Living Fountains

A living fountain requires some maintenance throughout the year to ensure that it continues to bring serenity and beauty to the garden. Floating pond plants require little care, other than scooping out the excess plants when overgrown and occasionally removing any decaying or yellowing leaves. Most are tropical plants and therefore won't tolerate a frost, so where winters are cold they should be treated like annuals: replaced each year or propagated indoors.

Your living fountain will naturally have organic debris that will go into the pump. Keep the water clean by changing it throughout the

season and giving the pump a good flushing once in a while to clear it out. To flush the pump, set it in a bucket of clean water and run it for an hour. Change the water and run again as many times as needed to clean the pump. Use a toothbrush to scrub the pump clean if necessary. Never leave the pump in water to freeze.

FLOATING AQUATIC PLANTS

Floating aquatic plants are striking in their own right and are a good choice for planting in a fountain or other small water feature, as they don't require much space. Consider some of the following choices:

Fairy moss (*Azolla caroliniana*). This rapid spreader is sometimes called "mosquito fern," because its fernlike foliage will quickly cover the water's surface, preventing mosquitoes from finding a place to lay their eggs.

Frogbit (*Hydrocharis morsus-ranae*). The leaves of frogbit look similar to water lilies but send up less-decorative white flowers.

Sensitive plant (*Neptunia aquatica*). So named because the fern-like leaves close when touched, sensitive plant has sweet pea–like yellow flowers.

Water fern (*Salvinia natans*). The fuzzy, fernlike leaf of this plant has a decorative shape similar to an accordion. The texture and the way the water beads on the leaves make this a good choice for a decorative plant.

Water hyacinth (*Eichhornia crassipes*). These quirky, bulblike plants with rubbery, deep-green leaves are decorative on their own, but if the conditions are right they will send out purple flowers as well. They tend to like standing water best, so fountain living may deter flowering. However, the leaves and shape are so attractive that they are still worth considering. (SEE PHOTO: 1.)

Water lettuce (*Pistia stratiotes*). The fuzzy, gray-green leaves of water lettuce create decorative rosettes on the water's surface and will quickly multiply. (SEE PHOTO: 2.)

NOTE: Since many floaters spread rapidly, they may also be characterized as invasive in some areas. Even if plants are for sale at your local garden center, check whether or not it is locally invasive and avoid planting if it is.

RECYCLED FENCE
BOARD SCONCES

1

2

IN MY NEIGHBORHOOD THERE WAS

an old farmhouse that sat atop a hill and looked down to what was once farmland in all directions. When the owners passed on and their family sold the property to developers, the neighbors came out to shed a tear and share memories of the house that was beautifully decrepit, remembered, and loved. We were allowed to collect a few items from the huge heap of debris that the house had become. I chose the fence boards that surrounded the garden. The boards that the raspberry and blackberry bushes spilled over, offering fruit to those who passed by. The boards that contained the vegetable garden that I would visit regularly to learn the tricks that made it so fruitful.

While to some the fence boards may have looked like nothing more than shabby, battered pieces of wood, I honored the beauty of the farmhouse by turning them into art. I brushed off the dirt and gave them a quick sanding, but left the nail holes and layers of paint, careful not to remove their character. With some simple construction, the boards have now become candle sconces, hanging on my own fence. When I light the candles and entertain late into the night, I'm reminded of the value of history and neighbors, and I hope that this little token of that farmhouse helps the memories live on.

You certainly do not need materials with such a history to make this project special. Wood in any case has the history of the tree it once was, and it surely has beauty in its grain. This project would look as at home indoors as out, perhaps as sconces on either side of a window. Choose wood that is meaningful to you, and the project will light a memory with every flicker of the candle.

MATERIALS

Found fence boards, barn wood, or
    other decorative wood in a size
    that fits your project (see Note)
Sandpaper (80 grit)
Tape measure
Pencil

Square
Table saw
Wood glue
Clamps
Picture-hanging hardware
Screwdriver

NOTE: For this project the total precut size of the ¾-inch-thick fence boards are 2½ inches wide by 20 inches long. This is a good size for a tea light sconce. Use wider boards for larger candles and vases. You may also use boards that are half an inch thick, but no thinner.

INSTRUCTIONS

Remove all nails from recycled boards, and sand any loose paint or rough edges. (SEE PHOTO: 1.)

Measure three and a half inches from the bottom of the board and draw a straight line across the front of the board using a square and pencil. Use a table saw to cut off the end of the board at the line. This piece will be the shelf of the sconce. The longer piece remaining will be the back of the sconce. (SEE PHOTOS: 2, 3.)

3

Measure about four inches from the bottom of the long board, about one-quarter of the total length. Use the square again to draw a straight line across the board. From that line, measure up the thickness of the board; for this project it is three-quarters of an inch. Draw a straight line across the board. You will now have two parallel lines; one 4 inches from the bottom and the other 4¾ inches from the bottom. This is where you will cut a groove so you can insert the sconce shelf into the sconce back. *Note:* you will want a tight fit, so when measuring it is best to err on the side of being too narrow rather than too wide.

4

Set the height of your table saw blade to be one half inch. Ensure you are cutting a groove into the sconce back and not cutting all the way through. Line up the bottom line so that the saw blade will pass to just inside the line (once again, you want to err on making the groove too narrow rather than too wide). Run the sconce back over the saw repeatedly while staying within the marked lines. As you get closer to the other line, you should check before each new cut to see if the sconce shelf will fit snugly within the groove. (SEE PHOTOS: 4, 5.)

5

When your groove is the right size so that the shelf fits in nicely, use wood glue to permanently affix the shelf. Run a bead of wood glue in the groove and spread it around so it coats the entire groove. Insert the shelf and clamp it. Wipe off any extra glue and allow to fully dry. (SEE PHOTO: 6.)

6

Add hanging hardware appropriate for the size of the sconce you have made. To hold a tea light, simple picture-hanging hardware will do. If you intend for the sconce to hold a heavier item or something breakable, use more secure hardware. (SEE PHOTO: 7.)

7

FOUR ELEMENTS
CANDLE TROUGH

BALANCE IS IMPORTANT IN THE

garden. Wherever possible, I try to vary elements, heights, and shapes when planning my outdoor spaces. Clumps of orderly grasses and uniform structure become more personal with a few delicate flowers thrown into the mix. Floppy, old-fashioned perennials add a little romance to a formal bed. And don't underestimate the power of a kitschy garden sculpture amid some well-tended shrubs. Balance invites visitors, provides comfort, inspires conversation, and shows off your personality.

This candle trough balances four elements: cool concrete, sparkling water, flickering fire, and floating blooms. It makes a lovely centerpiece to a long picnic table, and its movement encourages energy to be shared among those who gather around.

1

MATERIALS

Repair concrete (see Note)

Wheelbarrow or large bucket

Trowel

Long plastic tray at least 3" deep

Cardboard box or smaller plastic tray

Duct tape

Gravel or stones (for weight)

Vegetable oil

Foam brush

Gloves

Plastic drop cloth

Floating candles

NOTE: Choose a lightweight concrete mix (less gravel) for a smoother finished product. The best concrete for small, decorative projects is a repair concrete, which has no large pieces of gravel in it.

INSTRUCTIONS

Prepare the concrete in a wheelbarrow or large bucket by following the manufacturer's instructions.

Hunt around for two forms to make up the shape of the candle trough: a long plastic tray or container for the outer form and smaller container for the inner form. A seed starting tray and a cardboard box were used for this project. If using cardboard, cover the portion that will be exposed to the concrete in duct tape to prevent the concrete from

2

3

4

sticking. Weigh down the inner form by filling it with gravel, stones, or bricks.

Oil the forms well with the foam brush. (SEE PHOTO: 1.)

Fill the outer tray half full with concrete and shake to level it. (SEE PHOTO: 2.)

Press the cardboard box or inner form into the concrete to make a depression in the center. Press evenly and slowly. Go no farther than an inch and a half from the bottom of the tray. Smooth the concrete with a gloved hand or trowel to level it. Add more concrete if necessary to bring the sides up to the top of the outer tray. (SEE PHOTO: 3.)

Cover the project in a plastic drop cloth and leave to dry undisturbed for twenty-four hours. When the concrete is dry, remove the candle trough from the forms and cure according to the instructions on the concrete packaging. (SEE PHOTO: 4.)

Fill the candle holder with water, then add floating candles, flowers, and leaves to make a balanced centerpiece for a long table. (SEE PHOTO: 5.)

5

MODERN
GARDEN PLANTERS

CONCRETE DYE IS A FUN WAY TO

personalize modern planters by adding some color variation that mimics the layers of the earth. For this project I choose a rusty brown and deep charcoal dye to create the organic waves in the center of the planter. The lines echo the layers of the soil below, as if you can peek below the surface at what is surrounding the roots. You would never guess that the modern shapes that make up these upscale planters come from yogurt tubs, cups, and other plastic containers. Head on out to your recycling bin and see what shapes you can dig up!

The best plants for concrete are drought-tolerant succulents and plants that like soil with a higher pH. If the soil area is fairly small be sure to water regularly during the hot summer months. I generally avoid planting edibles in concrete in case of chemical leeching, but ornamental plants seem unaffected. As long as concrete planters are protected from freezing, they offer the benefit of overwintering plants right in the pot, as the roots will be better protected from the elements.

MATERIALS

Repair concrete (see Note)

Wheelbarrow or large bucket

Trowel

Collection of plastic containers in various sizes and shapes

¾" PVC pipe

Handsaw

Concrete dye (brown and charcoal used in this project) (see Resources)

Vegetable oil

Foam brush

Gloves

Bricks

Stones

Screwdriver

NOTE: Choose a lightweight concrete mix (less gravel) for a smoother finished product. The best concrete for small, decorative projects is a repair concrete, which has no large pieces of gravel in it.

INSTRUCTIONS

Prepare the concrete in a wheelbarrow or large bucket by following the manufacturer's instructions.

Select plastic containers in different shapes to create the planters. You'll need at least two containers per planter: one for the outer form and one for the inner form.

Oil the forms well with the foam brush. Be sure to oil the inside *and* outside of any forms you intend to use.

To use these planters outdoors, drainage holes are needed. Cut PVC pipe with a handsaw to a length that will create a hole from the inner container to the outer one. To do this, measure how deep you want the hole for your planter to go and cut the PVC pipe to that length. Use the trowel to add a layer of concrete to the outer form and press the PVC pipe in. The pipe will stay in the planter when it's completed, but if there is any concrete plugging up the hole, use a screwdriver to pop it out. (SEE PHOTOS: 1, 2, 3.)

To add layers of color to the project, mix concrete with dye in separate containers and layer colored concrete between layers of natural concrete. To remove air bubbles and level the concrete, tap the container rather than spreading the concrete to avoid the colors blending together. (SEE PHOTOS: 4, 5, 6.)

Cover the project in a plastic drop cloth and leave to dry undisturbed for twenty-four hours. When the concrete is dry, remove the forms and cure according to the instructions on the concrete packaging.

1

2

3

4

5

6

HARVESTING
ENGLISH LAVENDER

LAVENDER IS BY FAR MY VERY

favorite scent. I love it fresh when the plants are in bloom, as it dries around the garden, in sachets tucked into my pillow at night, or as bath salts when I soak away the aches of the gardening day. This magical herb is said to promote relaxation, relieve stress, and even soothe an achy head. Oh, and the bees love it, too. We can't forget the bees.

There are many different varieties of lavender, grown for ornamental appeal, fragrance, culinary uses, and drying. English lavender (*Lavandula angustifolia*) has delicate flowers on long stems that soar above the woody evergreen plant. French lavender (*Lavandula dentata*) and Spanish lavender (*Lavandula stoechas*) have showy bracts on bushy shrubs that excel as long-blooming garden additions. I grow a few ornamental lavender plants, but for year-round use, it's English all the way.

1

MATERIALS

English lavender plants ready for harvest (see Note)

Clean, sharp bypass pruners

Garden twine

Large bowl

Glass container with lid

NOTE: The best time to harvest English lavender is when the buds have formed on the plant but the flowers have not yet opened. Lavender harvested at this time of year will fall off the stems more easily when dry. The particular variety, or cultivar, of lavender will determine the fragrance, color, and longevity of its dried properties: *Lavandula angustifolia* 'Hidcote', *Lavandula x intermedia* 'Grosso', and *Lavandula x intermedia* 'Provence' are good varieties for drying.

2

INSTRUCTIONS

Harvest lavender with sharp bypass pruners and gather a small handful of long flower stems. Snip them at the base and continue collecting stems in your hand until you have a nice-sized bundle. Secure the bundle with twine and continue gathering bundles until the plant is fully harvested. (SEE PHOTOS: 1, 2.)

Pruning the plants like this will keep the shrub tidy and evergreen

3

4

5

through some colder climates. If your plants are leggy and you see an abundance of dead wood, it's a good idea to summer prune them each year until they regain a tidier shape.

Dry lavender in a warm, dry location out of direct sunlight: under eaves, in the garage, or somewhere in the garden that is protected. After two to four weeks it should be fully dried and you can shake or gently rub the flower buds into a tray or bowl. Store lavender in a lidded jar in a cool dark place. Repeat annually. (SEE PHOTOS: 3, 4, 5.)

LAVENDER SACHETS

Scoop lavender into small muslin bags with drawstrings—the kind typically sold in cooking stores as bouquet garni bags (for adding herbs to soups, stocks, or stews). Tie the bag tightly in a few knots and then wrap the string around the top and tie again. Add sachets to drawers and closets as a natural fabric freshener. Tuck one into your pillow and enjoy the heavenly scent as you snooze. Toss a bag in the dryer with laundry to add a light fragrance. Used as a dryer bag, the sachet will freshen up to ten loads of laundry.

MASON JAR
SOLAR LANTERNS

——

THE GARDEN IS A MAGICAL PLACE

at night. There is a whole new world that comes alive, one that is a little more rough-and-tumble. Nocturnal creatures like rodents, raccoons, owls, and bats venture out—as do critters like fireflies, beetles, and slugs. These are the visitors that hunt in our gardens, despite the fact that we don't often see them. They wear dark masks and sneak around in the shadows. Our gardens are their playgrounds at night.

There are a number of night-blooming plants that open or release fragrance only in the evening to attract special pollinators like moths, bats, or evening-foraging bees. Setting out a few mason jar lanterns in the garden can light up the pathways and invite you to explore the garden after dark, if you dare!

MATERIALS

Mason jar with ring (see Note)

Stake solar light (see Note)

Frosted-glass spray paint (see Resources)

Double-sided foam tape

16-gauge wire

Wire cutters

NOTE: There are many different sizes of solar stake lights available, and you may have to adjust the sizes based on what you can source. For this project, I used stake lights from a grocery store that I purchased for two dollars each. The light, solar panel, and battery are all contained in the top part, which simply unscrews from the plastic base. This part was just shy of the 78mm (about 3 inches) mouth of the vintage canning jars I had. Most modern canning jars are sold in regular mouth (70mm; 2¾ inches) or wide mouth (86mm; 3⅖ inches), so look for lights with dimensions a hair smaller than those if you are using standard jars.

INSTRUCTIONS

Frosting the mason jar gives the light a moonlike glow and a finished look. Shake the glass-frosting paint well and apply a light coat to the inside of the jar according to the manufacturer's instructions. Allow the paint to dry completely before applying subsequent coats. Keep frosting the glass until you are happy with the opacity. (SEE PHOTO: 1.)

1

Remove the stake from the solar light. If your solar light is a fraction smaller than the mason jar ring, a piece of double-sided foam tape wrapped around the solar unit can help to adjust the size and allow it to fit snugly in the mouth of the jar. Leave the backing on the tape if you want to be able to remove and replace the light. Many lights have an on-off switch so you can conserve battery power when the lights are in storage. (SEE PHOTO: 2.)

To turn the mason jar light into a mason jar lantern, add a hanging wire. Cut a 16-inch length of wire and twist a loop in the center. Wrap the two ends of the wire around the mason jar ring and twist them into a second loop on the other side of the ring. Snip off any extra wire. (SEE PHOTOS: 3, 4.)

Cut a second 16-inch length of wire and thread both ends through the loops on either side of the canning jar ring. (SEE PHOTO: 5.)

Set the lanterns in the sun for four to eight hours to charge, then hang them wherever you want to light up the night. (SEE PHOTOS: 6, 7, 8.)

2

3

4

5

THE NIGHT GARDEN

Spice up the night with a garden full of plants that flower or release fragrance in the evening. The lists of plants that follow are adapted by Judy Sedbrook of the Colorado State University Cooperative Extension Master Gardener Program.

Night-Flowering Plants

Evening primrose (*Oenothera* species): With sweetly scented blossoms of soft white, pink, and bright yellow that open in the evening, this fast-spreading perennial is hardy in zones 5–9.

Moonflower (*Ipomoea alba*): This night-blooming relative of the morning glory perfumes the garden as its large five-to-six-inch white flowers open at dusk. It is a quick-growing climber with large heart-shaped leaves.

Angel's trumpet (*Datura innoxia*): Huge six-inch white flowers appear from midsummer until frost on this viney annual, opening at night and remaining open well into the following day. They have a delicious fragrance, especially in the evening. The plant grows

6

7

8

three to four feet tall and wide with an abundance of blue-green foliage. *Warning:* This plant is poisonous and should be kept away from children.

Night phlox (*Zaluzianskya capensis*): During the day, flowers on these upright growing plants (also known as "midnight candy") are tightly closed. As dusk comes on, they open, releasing a honey-almond-vanilla fragrance.

Night-scented stock (*Matthiola longipetala*): The small white to purplish flowers of this plant are not showy, but they emit an intoxicating fragrance at night. Night-scented stock grows to one foot tall and has lance-shaped leaves.

Four o'clocks (*Mirabilis jalapa*): These sweetly fragrant and colorful trumpet-shaped flowers open in late afternoon, releasing a jasmine-like perfume.

Nottingham catchfly (*Silene nutans*): With a scent that is reminiscent of hyacinths, flowers of this plant open on three successive nights before fading. They are native to England.

Night-blooming cereus (*Selenicereus* species): This cactus, known for its large, fragrant, night-blooming white flowers, is not hardy at temperatures below 55 degrees Fahrenheit, but it can be grown in containers and brought indoors for winter.

Daylilies (*Hemerocallis* species): Many types of daylilies bloom at night, including *Hemerocallis* 'Moon Frolic' and *Hemerocallis* 'Toltec Sundial'.

Yucca (*Yucca filamentosa*): The flowers of this plant are open all day, but at night the blossoms lift and release their soapy fragrance.

Night-Fragrant Plants

Flowering tobacco (*Nicotiana* species): The long, trumpetlike blooms of this lovely annual are valued for their intense evening fragrance.

Night gladiolus (*Gladiolus tristis*): The creamy yellow blossoms have an intense spicy fragrance at night.

August lily (*Hosta plantaginea*): Waxy, trumpet-shaped flowers appear on thirty-inch stems; each flower is five inches long and three inches wide. The scent is of pure honey.

Fragrant columbine (*Aquilegia fragrans*): The creamy white flowers have a rich honeysuckle scent.

Pinks (*Dianthus plumarius*): The pale pink flowers have a rich clove scent.

Fairy lily (*Chlidanthus fragrans*): A few yellow, fragrant flowers bloom from each stalk in midsummer.

CITRONELLA CANDLES

IF YOUR FAVORITE THING IN THE

summer is spending warm nights outside, then likely one of your least favorite things is getting eaten alive by mosquitoes. Making citronella candles is a simple recycling project that is inexpensive and effective. I make plenty of candles to create a bug-free barrier around the patio so I can enjoy my warm breezes and summer cocktails in peace. They aren't bad for adding atmosphere either!

Citronella has a strong citrusy scent that can be overpowering. I add pine and mandarin orange essential oils in addition to citronella to make the fragrance more pleasant for people while still sticking it to the mosquitoes. The most effective candles will still be primarily citronella, but feel free to add a few other fragrances the bugs won't like, such as eucalyptus, rosemary, peppermint, and oregano.

MATERIALS

Hot glue gun

Cans, washed and with labels removed

6" wired wicks with tabs (see Resources)

Plastic straw

Double boiler

Wax (soy wax, paraffin wax, or old candles)

Citronella oil

Essential oils such as pine, mandarin orange, eucalyptus, peppermint (optional)

Chopsticks

Old towels

INSTRUCTIONS

Use hot glue to secure the wicks to the inside bottom of the cans. Thread the wick through a straw and press the tab of the wick firmly into the center. If you are using a large can, add two or three wicks spaced apart around the center. (SEE PHOTO: 1.)

Add wax or old candles in small pieces to a double boiler. Heat over medium heat until the wax is completely melted. (SEE PHOTO: 2.)

Now is the time to add oils for fragrance. Add one ounce of citronella oil per pound of wax, and augment with half an ounce of any other scents you are using, per pound of wax.

Let the wax cool slightly and carefully pour or ladle it into the containers. (SEE PHOTO: 3.)

Centering the wick is important for even burning. Hold the wick for a few seconds as the wax settles and it should stay in the center of the candle. If you are having difficulty keeping the wick in place, lay a chopstick across the top of the can to help prop the wick up on any side it is falling toward. Try not to tug or pull on the wick, as the hot glue will have been melted by the hot wax. The tab will stay in place as long as you don't fuss with it too much. (SEE PHOTO: 4.)

After pouring all of the candles, carefully group them together and wrap towels around the outside of the grouping. Cooling them slowly and completely will create the best-looking candles. If you get a depressed area around the wick once it is cooled, warm up some more wax and pour it into the void.

Allow the candles to cure for forty-eight hours undisturbed before burning. Then, when you fire a candle up, let it burn so that there is a full, wide pool of wax before you blow it out. It is said that candles have a memory, so it's best to let the first burn set the tone for all the rest.

1

2

3

4

CONTRIBUTED BY GENEVIEVE SCHMIDT
OF NORTH COAST GARDENING
(www.NorthCoastGardening.com)

There's little that spoils an outdoor gathering faster than a descending cloud of mosquitoes. While these bloodsucking beasties form an important base to the food chain, there's no reason to invite them to feast on your dinner guests. Luckily, there's a simple and natural solution: plant an attractive and fragrant bouquet of flowers and edible herbs around benches, pathways, and patios. When you brush against these plants, they release oils into the air that confuse and repel mosquitoes. Choose varieties with colorful foliage to add visual as well as olfactory interest. Here are my favorites:

Peppermint, including variegated mint (*Mentha × piperita* 'Variegata') and the divinely scented chocolate mint

Lavender, such as heat- and cold-tolerant 'Phenomenal' (*Lavandula × intermedia* 'Phenomenal') and variegated 'Silver Edge' (*Lavandula walvera* 'Silver Edge')

Basil, especially the more pungent lemon basil (*Ocimum × citriodorum*), lime basil (*Ocimum basilicum* 'Americanum'), and Thai basil (*Ocimum basilicum var. thyrsiflora*)

Catnip (*Nepeta cataria*)

Catmint, like the old garden favorite 'Six Hills Giant' (*Nepeta × faassenii* 'Six Hills Giant'), the compactly growing *Nepeta* 'Cat's Meow', and the white-blooming *Nepeta* 'Snowflake'

Lemon balm, both green (*Melissa officinalis*) and the golden-variegated *Melissa* 'Aurea'

Marigolds, among them the exuberantly striped heirloom 'Harlequin' (*Tagetes patula* 'Harlequin') or the ruffled 'Kilimanjaro White' (*Tagetes erecta* 'Kilimanjaro White')

Rosemary, particularly the upright 'Barbeque' (*Rosmarinus officinalis* 'Barbeque'), which has strong stems useful as skewers, and the vivid chartreuse *Rosmarinus* 'Gold Dust'

Eucalyptus, especially smaller varieties such as willow peppermint (*Eucalyptus nicholii*), which can be used as a patio tree

Citronella grass (*Cymbopogon nardus* or *Cymbopogon winterianus*)

TRASH-to-TREASURE
SOLAR CHANDELIER

EACH YEAR I ANTICIPATE THE

moment that my family can start eating our meals outdoors. While I have a dining room to use in the winter months, it feels more celebratory to swing open the French doors and dine on the deck. We magically extend our living space each year by adding a room with a view, fresh breezes, and the sounds of the neighborhood: birds chirping, children playing, dogs barking, and bikes whizzing by. Bringing indoor elements outdoors to furnish the space—like an outdoor rug, comfortable settee, and a chandelier—create the comfort you enjoy inside with the pleasures of being outside.

Whether you want to create an outdoor bedroom, living space, or dining room, this project takes a back alley find from trash to treasure. A neighbor's discarded light fixture was the inspiration for this solar light chandelier. A coat of bright paint and some hardware store stake lights turn it into a showpiece in the evening hours, providing a moonlike glow bathing the entertaining space and making it feel like part of my home.

MATERIALS

Chandelier (see Note)

Screwdriver

Wire cutters

Outdoor paint and primer
combination (see Note)

Paintbrush

Solar stake lights (see Note)

Silicone sealer

Galvanized wire (thin gauge)

Decorative beads and crystals

Needle-nose pliers

NOTE: There are enough old light fixtures in the world that the basis for this project should not be difficult to find. Try online ads, neighbors, thrift shops, or secondhand building supply shops for an inexpensive chandelier. Look for one with light sockets that face upward or that you can reassemble that way.

When selecting paint, make sure it is made to adhere to the material the chandelier is made of. You can choose a brush-on paint or spray paint. Brush-on paint is a bit more time consuming but color choices are endless; spray paint is easy to apply but colors are limited.

Purchase solar lights in a size that will fit into the light sockets on your chandelier. It's also helpful to find ones that can be disassembled easily. In the case of the stakes I used for this project, it simply meant removing the plastic ground stake for these pathway lights, leaving behind a light fixture that fit right into the socket. Lights with an on-off switch are handy, as you can turn them off when the light is in storage to conserve battery life. In general, inexpensive plastic solar lights will work just fine. Buy a few extra in case they need replacing down the road.

1

INSTRUCTIONS

Prepare the chandelier by removing all the parts you won't need, like the shades or wiring. (SEE PHOTOS: 1, 2.)

Paint any parts of the solar lights and the chandelier that you think will add to the overall look. Painting the tops of the solar lights brings the whole chandelier together cohesively. A bright sunny color makes this fixture as engaging in the day as it is in the evening. (SEE PHOTOS: 3, 4, 5, 6.)

Fill the sockets with silicone sealer and place the ends of the solar lights inside. Allow the silicone to dry completely. (SEE PHOTO: 7.)

2

To decorate your chandelier with beads or crystals, cut a six-inch length of galvanized wire in a thin enough gauge to fit through the hole in the bead or crystal. Thread a crystal through one end of the wire and use the needle-nose pliers to twist the wire together just above the crystal. Cut off the short end of the wire with your wire cutters and thread a bead or two onto the long end. Wrap the remaining wire around the arm of the chandelier and trim any extra wire. (SEE PHOTOS: 8, 9, 10.)

Hang the solar chandelier where the sun will charge the lights during the day, and lights will glow above your entertaining space in the night. (SEE PHOTO: 11.)

3

4

5

8

6

9

10

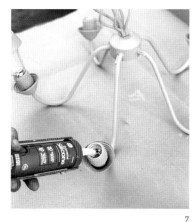

7

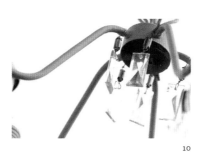

11

A summer night spent under the moon-like glow of a solar chandelier should be enjoyed with a delicious cocktail. Whether it's to sip in quiet enjoyment of a productive gardening day or a festive celebration with friends, this Moonlight Mojito is sure to satisfy.

MAKES 2 SERVINGS

6 mint sprigs
1 teaspoon grated fresh ginger
2 tablespoons sugar
Juice of 1 lemon
3 ounces dark rum
Ice
Soda water

Muddle the mint, grated ginger, and sugar with a mortar and pestle. Juice the lemon into the mortar and stir well. Add the mixture to a cocktail shaker with the rum and ice. Fill the shaker with soda, stir, and pour into cocktail glasses.

VINTAGE HIGH CHAIR SWING

TALK ABOUT BABYING YOUR PLANTS!

This vintage-high-chair-turned-hanging-plant-swing is a good reminder that a garden needs nourishment and care. For some, the idea of gardening is equivalent to hard work. Digging, planting, weeding, watering, pruning, and deadheading can seem like words of torture, but with a little planning you can create a garden that is more joy than job (see "Right Plant, Right Place"). For me, whimsical garden art like this repurposed high chair reminds me that the garden is my playground. Planning new plantings, cleaning up the beds, enjoying the cool mist of water as it sprays from the hose, shaping trees, and encouraging new growth are fulfilling activities that further beautify the space. Spending days filling terracotta pots with foliage and blooms to accent a decorative feature feeds the need for crafting and puts a smile on my face whenever I pass by.

NOTE: This design is not intended as seating for children or adults or for doing any actual swinging. It is, however, just the right spot for displaying plants, a bird feeder, or a birdbath, or perhaps even to serve as a perch for kitty to supervise the garden.

MATERIALS

Vintage high chair made from solid wood (see Note)

Drill

Wood glue or filler

Sandpaper

Paintbrushes

Outdoor paint and primer combination

Sisal rope ³⁄₈"

Masking tape

NOTE: Look for a chair to suit this project. In this case a vintage high chair had the right look, but any wooden chair with arms that can be drilled into and a base that sits directly below the arm rests will allow you to attach the rope and hang the chair as a swing. (SEE PHOTO: 1.)

1

Remove the legs from the high chair. As with all vintage pieces, check the joints and screws for integrity. Tighten up loose screws or replace them. Fill holes with wood glue or wood filler and reinforce any weak joints.

Sand and wipe all surfaces to prepare for painting. Outdoor latex paint will protect the wood, and if you use a paint and primer combination it will save you the step of priming the wood first. After two or three coats of paint, allow the chair to dry completely in a covered area away from direct sunlight. (SEE PHOTOS: 2, 3.)

Using a small drill bit, drill two holes in each arm of the chair, one near the front and the other close to the chair back. Then use a large-sized drill bit to make a larger hole, a size that easily allows the rope to fit through. (SEE PHOTO: 4.)

Use a thin paintbrush with a dab of paint to mark the bottom holes on the seat. Feed the paintbrush through the top hole, straight down to the seat. Mark where the bottom hole should be with the paint. (SEE PHOTO: 5.)

Drill the bottom holes as you did with the top holes. If it is difficult to drill from the top of the seat, drill a pilot hole from the top then flip the seat over and drill the larger holes from the bottom. (SEE PHOTOS: 6, 7.)

To hang the chair, run a length of rope through the top holes, then the bottom holes, and tie in a knot beneath the seat. If the rope begins to fray when cut, wrap masking tape around the cut end and it will feed through the holes more easily. Continue to tie all four sides and use the upper length of rope to secure the swing to a tree. (SEE PHOTOS: 8, 9, 10.)

2

3

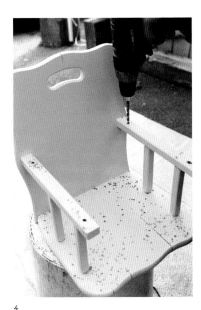

4

5

6

7

It is certainly possible to create a low-maintenance garden that brings as much enjoyment as a more labor-intensive version. The key is to choose the right plants for the right place. If you try to grow an apple tree in a patio planter, it will require a lot of attention to prune, fertilize, water, and transplant regularly. If apple trees were that much effort, then apples in the produce section would require a loan to purchase! Plant an apple tree in a sunny orchard with the right soil and enough room to spread out its branches, and the work of the year is much more limited.

Think about the "right plant, right place" rule when designing your garden. Build healthy soil and choose plant cultivars that are right for your garden's conditions: sunny or shady, moist or dry, acid or alkaline. If one kind of plant is not thriving in a bed where others are growing in leaps and bounds, consider removing that plant for good. If you find you are endlessly weeding, pack your garden with closely planted vegetables, perennials, bushes, and trees that will eventually crowd the weeds. If watering becomes a daily task, consider choosing drought-tolerant plants and a landscape design that requires little supplemental watering. These are some ways to ensure that your garden is a source of enjoyment for you, rather than an endless list of chores.

If the right place to hang this swing planter is under a tree, then the right plants are shade-loving plants. The plants used in this project get some direct sunlight for just a few hours a day, so leafy heuchera, sedum, and viola thrive in this yellow, lime green, and plum planting combination.

8

9

10

A varied collection of weathered and mossy terracotta pots are my favorite functional garden art pieces. Whether stacked in storage or dotted around the garden to fill in bare spots, terracotta is a decorative staple that will change and become more pleasing over time. A few simple tips will help you enjoy your pots for years to come:

Put a coffee filter in the bottom of pots before adding soil to prevent soil from leaking out the drainage hole.

Overwinter pots undercover and prevent them from freezing. Terracotta pots will absorb water that can freeze in cold climates. When it warms up and the water thaws, it will cause the pot to break apart.

Clean pots between plants by removing all soil, scrubbing with a stiff brush, and washing thoroughly.

In rainy seasons, do not use saucers. Set pots on bricks or wedges to allow free flow from the drainage hole.

In warm, dry seasons, water regularly and allow some water to gather in the saucer. It will be absorbed quickly.

Add character to brand new pots by brushing some yogurt on the outside to encourage the growth of mosses and giving them a more weathered look.

3

FALL

FALL IN THE GARDEN IS A HECTIC TIME,

or at least it seems that way after the lazy days of summer. There's plenty to do before the cold winter months. The garden is worn out, having worked tirelessly all spring and summer to grow, bloom, and fruit. It has done its job and is looking for a winter's rest. Leaves are turning brilliant colors and there are fascinating seedpods to be found. A tour around the garden at this time of year is a lesson in redefining beauty. The gardener's job now is a much bigger task; it's time to harvest the fruit, veggies, herbs, and flowers.

For me, fall is a reflection of all that has been accomplished in the year and a homage to the days spent creating and nurturing this bountiful garden space. With each snip of the pruners I'm grateful for the flowers that bloomed and left behind ornamental seed-pods. To spend time collecting what remains in fall is its own form of garden making.

The attractiveness of the garden in fall is meant to entice us. To encourage us to slurp down the sweetest and plumpest tomato and then save its seeds. To harvest seed heads, sprinkling the ripe seeds on our way through the garden. To plant showy trees with sweet berries and cultivate sunflowers with protein-rich seeds that will feed the birds for the winter. How many of the plants in a garden would thrive if it weren't for our intervention? We are the helping hand they need to continue their legacy.

The time has come to collect those exquisite leaves and flowers and preserve them. Perhaps pressing them for use in wall art or cards. Or collecting a full basket of stalks to make dried arrangements or a harvest wreath. In raking up the leaves or walking on a brisk fall day, I will often find acorns, pinecones, bracket mushrooms, and driftwood that beg to be included in a craft project. I keep a large collection plate in the house to add the ever-growing abundance of weird and wonderful found things. Spiky chestnut casings, interesting lichens, and even butterfly wings make for inspiring artistic muses.

Fall is a time to feast, to put up food for the winter, to share bountiful harvests with loved ones. Family-style dinners are on the menu, in homes decorated for the season, to use up both the edible and ornamental glut of garden goodies. Setting the table aglow with gourds bearing flames, greeting guests with silly "jack-o'-planterns," spooking trick-or-treaters with lifelike spiders sculptures, or forcing bulbs in order to enjoy them indoors are all ways to remember the garden this season, and remind you of the fun you have had together throughout the year.

VINTAGE
SILVER PLANTERS

———

PERHAPS YOU ARE PART OF THE

generation that registered for a china pattern and silver set for formal entertaining. Perhaps you are part of the generation that has had these treasures passed on but keeps them in storage, tarnished and chipped, not fully appreciated and no longer useful. It's such a shame that a pretty milk and sugar set no longer graces a tea party, but it doesn't mean the set can't still hold a prominent place on the table.

Planting succulents in vintage silver, pewter, and china makes for charming table centerpieces, thoughtful gifts, or garden decoration. Try setting wedding tables with clusters of mismatched sets that can be taken home by the guests. Plant Mom's favorite silver for a sentimental Thanksgiving gift. Tuck planters around the garden to delight and surprise visitors. All of these ideas ensure that the history lives on, even if you've gathered your collection from a thrift shop.

MATERIALS

Vintage silver pots (see Note)

Cactus and succulent soil mix

Various succulents

½" river stones, pebbles, or glass beads

NOTE: To create container gardens out of found pots you must first consider whether you plan to use them outdoors or inside. Succulents generally like to go almost completely dry between watering, so standing water in the bottom of a pot will likely cause its demise. Outdoor pots will need drainage holes to deal with rain and garden irrigation systems. (See the teapot planter project on pages 38–40 for instructions on drilling drainage holes.)

INSTRUCTIONS

Choose your pots, plants, and location. Many succulents like to be in bright light, out of direct afternoon or hot summer sun, but the plant label should tell you the right conditions for each plant.

Remove the succulent from the nursery pot and place it in the silver container. Fill in the spaces around the roots with a cactus soil mix, which is specially blended to have good drainage and the right mix of nutrients for these unique plants.

Top the soil with stones, pebbles, or beads to create a neutral background for the succulent to shine. Play with composition by using a number of different varieties of succulents in the same pot.

RELIABLE SUCCULENTS FOR CONTAINERS

CONTRIBUTED BY JACKI CAMMIDGE OF DROUGHT SMART PLANTS
(www.drought-smart-plants.com)

Succulents do well in all kinds of containers as they have shallow root systems and are tolerant of neglect. Tender succulents do best in bright sunlight or high filtered shade but cannot withstand frost, making them good choices for mild weather or indoors. Hardy succulents will not thrive if brought indoors for the winter; they need a gradual cool-down and a cold season to go dormant. Hardy succulents are great choices for outdoor plants in colder areas.

Ten Tender Succulents

Sedum calvifolia: Blue-lobed foliage

Echeveria elegans: One of the nicest blue species of *Echeveria*

Echeveria 'Perle Von Nürnberg': Pale mauve-blue spoon-shaped foliage

Aloe 'Black Gem': Small compact green with dark overtones

Aeonium haworthia 'Kiwi': Pale green in winter, turning to shades of mango and peach in warmer weather

x Pachyveria: Hybrids of *Echeveria* and *Pachyphytum* that have chubby looking leaves

x Sedeveria nussbaumerianum 'Coppertone': *Sedum* and *Echeveria* hybrids with a standout bronze color

Crassula rupestris: Small, pale blue stacked towers

Haworthia obtusifolium: Chubby, low-growing lime green rosettes

Senecio mandraliscae: Blue spiky foliage, for a stunning central focal point in a mixed planter

Ten Hardy Succulents

Jovibarba species: All very similar, tend to make a colony or carpet of tiny rosettes thickly covering the surface of the soil

Sedum pachyclados: Low-growing pale green notched rosettes

Sedum oreganum: Lime-green-tinged bronze puffy leaves on red stems

Sedum spurium 'John Creech': Smallest of all the *spurium* varieties, with fresh green-lobed leaves and pink flowers

Sedum glaucophyllum: Greeny blue low-growing rosettes

Sedum spathiphyllum 'Capo Blanco': White, highly pruinose foliage, mounding by habit

Sempervivum arachnoideum Hookeri: Pale green tinged with red in cooler temperatures

Sempervivum 'Maria Laach': Medium-sized black-tipped rosettes

Sempervivum 'Blue Boy': Medium-sized blue rosettes

Sempervivum octopodes: Brilliant lime green rosettes, tightly packed

SAVING HEIRLOOM
TOMATO SEEDS

SAVING HEIRLOOM TOMATO SEEDS

brings back memories of science class: beakers and safety goggles, anticipation and disgust, curiosity and pride. The seeds can't just be scooped out and dried; they need to be removed with all the slimy tomato guts and left to ferment. The yuck factor of fermenting these tiny seeds is about as fun of a science experiment as you can get, making it an ideal project to do with kids.

MATERIALS

Heirloom tomatoes	Pen or marker
Knife and spoon	Fine-mesh sieve
Mason jars and rings	Paper or glass plates or bowls
Paper towel	Coin envelopes

INSTRUCTIONS

The most important part of saving heirloom seeds is selecting the best fruit to begin with. Whether you are purchasing your tomatoes or have grown your own, you should look for the best visual example of a variety: ideal color, size, and shape. Ensure there is no disease or pest damage, and don't forget to taste them. Yummy tomatoes make seeds that make yummy tomatoes. (SEE PHOTO: 1.)

Gently cut your ripe tomato into sections. Grab a spoon and scoop out the seeds and the gel-like membrane that they are surrounded by. The whole glob goes right into the mason jar, so it's going to get a bit messy. Fill up each jar with about one-quarter to one-half cup of water, just enough to cover the goop. (SEE PHOTO: 2.)

Write the tomato variety on a piece of paper towel folded square, and secure it over the mouth of the jar by twisting on the ring. This allows for air to circulate to the mixture as it ferments, but also makes sure you don't forget the variety. (SEE PHOTOS: 3, 4, 5.)

Now set the mason jars someplace warm, and out of direct sunlight, where they won't be disturbed for a few days. Depending on the temperature, the fermentation could take two days to a week, so be prepared to stick around and keep an eye on them. (SEE PHOTO: 6.)

Within a few days the top of the liquid should have a grayish rim of scum, and even later, it will have a full cover of mold. At this point the seeds should have sunk to the bottom of the muck as well. Congratulations! This means that the fermentation process is complete. This is also great news because the jars are likely smelling quite awful by now. (SEE PHOTO: 7.)

Add another half cup or so of water to the jars to dilute the gunk and allow the viable seeds to sink to the bottom. Gently pour off the top layer of fermenty goodness and then strain the seeds into a fine-mesh sieve. (SEE PHOTO: 8.)

Place the strained seeds on a plate or bowl and set them back in the warm, dry place for a few days more to dry out. Make sure that you attach your paper towel cover/label to the seeds; it can be awfully disappointing to go through the process of fermenting seeds and then not know which varieties they are! (SEE PHOTO: 9.)

Once your seeds are dry, you can shuffle them into some handy little coin envelopes, label them, and store them in a cool, dry place until next spring. Voilà! You have graduated from science-class geek to a true heirloom tomato alumnus.

4

5

6

7

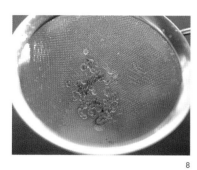

8

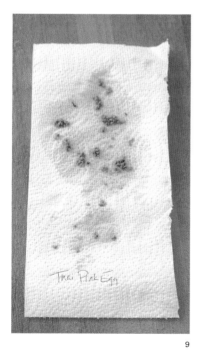

Thai Pink Egg

9

Heirloom seeds have been saved and passed on for many generations, and as such, the plant, flowers, and fruit are true to type of the original great-great-great-(insert fifty years here)-grandmother plant. The seeds have been saved for their outstanding qualities—for instance, beauty, flavor, yield, or resistance to disease, pests, and unfavorable weather conditions—which aren't necessarily the same qualities that are important in commercial agriculture (such as uniformity and sturdiness for shipping). Heirloom vegetables and fruits provide much-needed diversity from the standard fare mass-produced by industrial food producers.

Heirloom varieties not only offer colorful and unique alternatives to commercial tomato varieties, but they also enable growers to reliably propagate the (sometimes hard to find) seeds of their favorite old-fashioned varieties, rather than having to buy seeds every year. Hybrid tomatoes have been created by cross-pollinating strong characteristics of different varieties, making brand-spanking-new varieties. While the tomatoes can look and taste as good as heirlooms, saving these seeds comes with problems. When you germinate the hybrid seeds, there is no guarantee what characteristics the new plant will have. Remember, they cross-pollinated before, so it's anybody's guess what they will get up to with the other tomatoes and what the offspring will be.

FELTED ACORN MAGNETS

I REMEMBER ONE FALL DAY GIGGLING

to myself about a pocketful of acorn caps. I was, quite literally, squirreling away acorns for a project and had to pause to enjoy the humor of it all. I love to collect woodland items in the fall, so much so that my husband fondly nicknamed me "Squirrel" due to the number of items I accumulate day after day. I don't always know what the items will become, but the assortment of branches, nuts, and seed heads are inspiration for many a craft project on a cold and dreary day. On one of those days, my collection of acorn caps, along with puffs of colorful wool roving, got crafted into a set of charming fridge magnets.

Needle felting transforms fiber to sculpture right before your eyes. The act of stabbing a fluffy piece of wool with a very sharp, barbed needle causes the fiber to compact and tangle into a firm shape. This is sometimes called "dry felting," as opposed to the traditional method of wet felting that uses water and friction. Felted acorns are a wonderful first felting project, as you need only to make a simple round nut to sit beneath the acorn cap. With practice and experimentation, you will one day be able to make anything you can imagine, from rabbits to robots.

Before you begin, just a quick note on safety: A felting needle is surprisingly sharp, so try to avoid catching a finger under one. You will undoubtedly get poked a few times in the process (or perhaps you are more restrained than I am?), but please use care as you work. Regardless, this can be a family-friendly craft for older children, as long as instruction and supervision (and bandages) are available.

MATERIALS

Wool roving (see Resources)

Needles for felting or a needle-felting tool (see Resources)

Needle-felting mat or thick piece of foam (see Resources)

Acorn caps

Round magnets (see Resources)

Hot glue gun

Start by separating a piece of wool from the roving. Pull off a strip that is the width and length of a standard pencil. Pull the wool apart rather than cutting it, so the fibers remain intact. (SEE PHOTO: 1.)

Loosely wind the wool around itself. Place the wool on a felting mat and use the needle to jab the wool repeatedly on all sides. With a small project like this, one needle will work just fine, but a needle-felting tool that holds multiple needles will speed up a larger job. (SEE PHOTOS: 2, 3.)

Keep poking the wool at different angles, which draws the fibers into an organized tangle that compacts the shape and holds it together firmly. Continue turning and jabbing, while occasionally rolling the ball between your palms to smooth down the fibers. The finished project should feel firm from all sides and be the size and shape that you think will work well under an acorn cap. If you have any unsightly dimples or lumps, pull off more strands of wool and wrap the strands around the ball, filling the divots with thicker strands and using the needle to fill in the spaces with new wool and improve the shape. (SEE PHOTO: 4.)

Take some time to experiment with different shapes; needle felting more heavily in some areas will adjust the shape to create an egg, a tear-drop, a kidney, and other forms. For this project a ball works wonderfully, but it doesn't need to be perfect. Acorns come in many different shapes after all!

When you have a wool nut that you are happy with, search your acorn collection for a cap that fits well. If the caps are too large, then wind a bit of extra wool around the nut and felt some more. If the cap is too small, then compact the fibers with (you guessed it) more felting. (SEE PHOTO: 5.)

Use hot glue to attach the cap, and then again to glue the magnet on the back of the felted nut. It will dry in a minute, so go grab some artwork to post on the fridge! (SEE PHOTOS: 6, 7, 8.)

5

6

7

Do you wonder if the squirrels in your garden remember where they stashed all those nuts in the fall? Or if the squirrel digging up the nut is even the same one that buried it? Joel Brown from the University of Illinois at Chicago set up experiments to track the Eastern gray squirrel to show that yes, squirrels do know their caches, and yes, the same puffy-tailed critter who digs up a cache is the one who buried it. Squirrels are territorial, so the good news is that there are a limited number digging in your garden. The bad news is that if you dig up a cache and replant your garden, Mr. Squirrel will be back looking for it when he's hungry and your plants will be excavated in the process. If those wily critters drive you nuts with their very different ideas for designing your garden, the best defense is a pet offense: a resident dog or cat is the best deterrent for keeping squirrels out.

8

mores and history itself are reflected in garden style, just what a garden is, and what we want of our gardens today. Miss Fairbrother has an interesting mind and an adroit pen, and the journey her readers take through the Dark Ages and their monastic ones, the Middle Ages and their romantic ones, ... for England, and the formal ... eighteen-century England, is ... her as a guide.

... Buckner Hollingsworth *Her Garden* ... Macmillan ... promising ... break new ground by ... little known women gardeners, botanists, bot... ...ors, and garden writers who have played ... ... history of this country. The author's ... Geoffrey Taylor's, but whereas Dr. T... ... Victorian or ... and devotes more ... portrai... ...memoirs of just four ... his fi... ...ns, William Robinson, t... ... den re... ...ald Farrer, the gifted and ec- centric plant... ...s. Hollingsworth covers the field from ... ...ys to the very near past, and gives ... ...graphical sketches of women whose ... ...07 to 1863. The brevity is not the ... lot of research has gone into this ... with pleasant and surprising results, but when I had finished reading it I had the slightly uneasy feeling that in the early biographies there had been too little source material to flesh out the bare bones of fact, and that the American women gardeners who came later, about whom

PRESSED LEAF CARDS

IT'S HARD TO LET GO OF SUMMER.

If you live in an area where seasons are distinct, then four times each year you anticipate and grieve the coming of a new season. At the end of summer there is relief that the long, hot days are relenting to cooler fall temperatures even as you miss barefoot days in the garden and warm nights on the deck. Before the blooms fade, the pods pop open, and the leaves fall, it is an ideal time to collect nature's art supplies. These pressed leaf cards are a lovely way to send a little piece of your garden to those you love. Using vintage garden book pages as the matting adds a whimsical touch.

MATERIALS

Pressed dried leaves, flowers, and seeds (see "Pressing Leaves and Flowers")

Vintage garden-themed book pages

Card stock

Scissors and ruler, or paper trimmer

Blank cards and envelopes

Glue tape

White glue

Foam brush

Heavy book

INSTRUCTIONS

Choose a card stock color that coordinates with the dried flowers, leaves, or seeds that you want to use. Cut the card stock into a rectangle just a wee bit smaller than your blank card. Use the glue tape (a double-sided tape in a roll-on dispenser) to affix it to the card, so that the paper doesn't warp from the moisture in regular glue. Cut a book page to slightly smaller than the card stock and use the glue tape to affix it to the card stock. (SEE PHOTO: 1.)

Lay out the design for your cards. When you are happy with the look, use a foam brush to apply glue to the back of the plant material. Gently press the plant onto the book page and put a heavy book on top while it dries for twenty-four hours. (SEE PHOTO: 2.)

Decorate your cards further if you wish, with paint or pen, before scribing a message to a loved one and mailing it off. (SEE PHOTOS: 3, 4.)

1

2

3

To preserve tender leaves and vivid petals, harvest them at their peak of color and place them on pages of an old telephone book or on newspaper; set heavy books on top as weights. Newsprint is absorbent and provides plenty of space to dry flowers.

4

AUTUMN HARVEST
WREATH

IT ALL COMES DOWN TO THIS:

harvest. The time of the gardening year when all you have planted and nurtured has reached its peak of color, flavor, and beauty. Those long hot days are slowing down, the sun gleams lower in the sky, and leaves take on warm hues of gold, orange, and red. If you have been gardening all year you very well may have a bounty to contend with. Drying is a great preservation option for the gathered garden goodies you can't make into jam or store in the freezer. This autumn harvest wreath bundles both ornamental and edible delights and allows them to dry in a way that is so beautiful it can grace the front door.

MATERIALS

Grapevine wreath

Bypass pruners

Freshly cut herbs and flowers
   (see Note)

Dried seed heads (see Note)

Garden twine

NOTE: Plants shown in this project include the following: (SEE PHOTO: 1.)

   Top row, left to right: *Celosia, limonium, Eryngium planum,* garden sage (*Salvia officinalis*), daylily (*Hemerocallis species*) seedpods, Russian hardneck garlic (*Allium sativum ophioscorodon*).

   Bottom row, left to right: *Lunaria annua* seed heads, *Nigella damascena* seed heads, *Juncus ensifolius* seed heads, *Papaver somniferum* seed heads.

INSTRUCTIONS

Cut herbs and blossoms when they look their very best: lush and unblemished. It's good practice to harvest in the morning on a clear day, after the dew has evaporated but before the hot, afternoon sun blazes. (SEE PHOTOS: 1, 2.)

   When cutting fresh flowers or herbs to use in this wreath, cut twice as much as you think you will need, to account for shrinking as the plants dry. I chose sage for the base of this wreath because of how the leaves turn silvery green and curl as they dry. For a greener wreath,

1

2

choose a broadleaf evergreen—such as a laurel or magnolia—as your base.

Collect a varied selection of decorative seed heads for this project to really celebrate the abundance that the garden provides. Not just in blooms and edibles but in decorative crafting materials as well.

To create the wreath, gather a bouquet of flowers and greens in your hand and tie them to the grapevine wreath with garden twine. The bouquet should have a nice selection of greenery at the back with the more decorative elements layered on top. You can add more delicate seed heads at this time, but hardneck garlic and seed heads with strong stems will be added at the end. Keep one end of your twine long so that you can tie bunch after bunch onto the wreath form. (SEE PHOTO: 3.)

Gather a second bouquet and layer it over the first, covering the twine. Continue to add bouquets until you have tucked the very last stems under the first blooms you added. Tie the twine securely and snip the ends. (SEE PHOTOS: 4, 5, 6.)

Now stand back and have a look at the overall shape. Use your pruners to clip busy or straggling bits and add more plant material to the wreath to fill in bare spots. The firm-stemmed plants can be added at this stage. Cut the stems to three to five inches long and add them to the wreath by tucking them under the twine. This will tighten the twine and create a firmer hold on the plant material. (SEE PHOTOS: 7, 8.)

If you are adding fresh herbs and flowers to your wreath, gravity will cause them to droop as they dry. Turn your wreath every day to ensure the plants dry in an even shape. There's nothing to say that you can't continue to prune or add to your wreath as it changes and, perhaps, as more beautiful things are ready to be harvested in your garden. (SEE PHOTO: 9.)

Hang your wreath in a warm, dry, airy place away from the sun. A shady front door is just the right spot. (SEE PHOTO: 10.)

3

4

5

6

7

8

9

10

Flowers leave behind interesting seedpods and dried stalks that are wonderful for crafts. Don't be too hasty with the pruners in the fall, as many species that dry in the garden can be easily picked later in the season. Remember, it's the plant's job to multiply by spreading the seeds trapped in that fancy pod, so keep a close eye on them as they mature. When the petals have fallen away and the seed head looks sturdy, it's time to collect them—before the elements break down the pod and scatter the seeds. If necessary, dry seed heads further by grouping them into bunches and hanging them upside down, either outdoors (away from both rain or direct sunlight) or protected indoors.

ORNAMENTAL
GOURD TEA LIGHTS

1

2

3

4

SQUASH ARE ENTHUSIASTIC GROWERS.

If you have ever composted squash seeds you know those suckers are probably going to grow somewhere in your garden next year. It could be right in the compost pile, or perhaps one snuck its way into the flower bed. Regardless, the plant is going to make a concerted effort to give you some squash.

At this point you are probably saying to yourself, "What's the problem? Growing volunteer squash sounds fabulous!" It is fabulous, if you like surprises. All varieties look the same until they fruit, more or less, so it will be difficult to know if the plant will produce the yummy butternut you made into soup or the haunting blue pumpkin that you displayed at the front door. Even if you can figure out what seeds have volunteered, there is a chance it will not look and taste like the parent you remember (see "Squash: Know Your Lineage").

I love surprises. When I see a squash peeking out of my strawberry bed, I treat it with love and hope for something delicious. Last year, however, I nurtured a few guest plants and when harvest time came around, the bed was full of ornamental gourds. I must say I was a bit disappointed I couldn't eat the fruits of my labor. Recovering quickly, I untucked the napkin from my collar and got busy turning those cuties into tea light holders. They redeemed themselves quickly.

MATERIALS

Ornamental gourds with
    flat bottoms

Serrated knife
Tea lights

INSTRUCTIONS

To make ornamental gourd tea lights, use a sharp serrated knife to cut out a candle-sized hole in the top of the gourd. Insert tea light and enjoy. (SEE PHOTOS: 1, 2, 3.)

Bonus points for hollowing out the inside of a gourd, adding a bit of potting soil, and planting flowers. (SEE PHOTO: 4.)

Squash are the freewheeling hippies of the vegetable world. Unless you have an heirloom variety (as discussed in "Saving Heirloom Tomato Seeds"), the fruit of a squash plant is the product of its mother (seed) and father (pollen from another plant). Squash don't discriminate much between types of pollen, and the seeds can be fertilized by just about any other squash plant, even a melon! The current year's fruit will retain the traits it was intended to have, but if the seeds sneak their way into next year's garden, they could have the traits of either parent, or you might even grow a completely weird (and maybe yummy) new kind of squash. To ensure you get the squash you bargained for, only plant seeds from a trusted source or saved seeds from heirloom varieties.

MASON JAR
FORCED BULBS

———

BULB FORCING HAS BEEN A GARDENER'S

pastime since the 1800s. If you are an antiques hunter, you may have seen hyacinth glasses or forcing vases: pinched-neck glass vases with wide bottoms. Perhaps you have seen more current displays of fragrant paperwhites set in soil at a florist shop. The hobby's longevity is understandable when you come to appreciate that spring's fragrant blooms can be grown right on your windowsill, in the fall! Forced bulbs provide a fresh, long-lasting display of bright green leaves atop a growing bulb that is decorative enough in its own right, even before the flowers appear. Here are three different ways to create gorgeous mason jar forced bulbs: in soil, in pebbles, and in water.

1

MATERIALS

FOR FORCING BULBS IN SOIL

Quart-sized or larger mason jar

Clean ½" diameter stones

Indoor potting soil mix

Paperwhite bulbs

FOR FORCING BULBS IN PEBBLES

Wide, pint-sized mason jar with a
    regular-sized mouth

Clean ½" diameter stones

Prechilled hyacinth bulbs (*Hyacinth*
    'Delft Blue' shown)

FOR FORCING BULBS IN WATER

Wide, pint-sized mason jar with a
    regular-sized mouth

Plastic mesh

Garden twine

Prechilled hyacinth bulbs (*Hyacinth*
    'L'Innocence' shown)

2

INSTRUCTIONS

Forcing Bulbs in Soil

Planting bulbs in soil is the most obvious choice and makes for a stable base for tall flowers like paperwhites. Start with a clean mason jar and line the bottom with an inch of half-inch diameter stones. Top the stones with a few inches of soil and set a bulb in so that the neck is above the soil line. Pack soil around the bulb and press firmly in place. (SEE PHOTOS: 1, 2, 3.)

3

Unlike plant pots, mason jars don't have drainage holes. They do have front-row viewing to the root system, though, so monitoring watering is quite simple. Water to moisten the soil but not so much that there is standing water at the bottom of the jar. If you add too much water you can always pour it back out. Keep an eye on the roots: they should be white and long, winding through the soil in the jar. Being able to see below the surface adds to the charm of the container and it makes a great learning project for kids. (SEE PHOTO: 4.)

4

Forcing Bulbs in Pebbles

Fill the jar to just an inch below the neck with clean stones, glass beads, or decorative marbles. Nestle the bulb on the top of the stones, using a few extras to secure the bulb in place. Add water to just half an inch below the surface. (SEE PHOTOS: 5, 6.)

5

Forcing Bulbs in Water

To force bulbs in water, create a hammock out of plastic mesh to allow the bulb to sit above the water line. Shown in the photos here is the packaging from the decorative stones I used in the pebble-forcing method, but you could also use purchased mesh or the packaging often used with onions and avocados. Use the bulb to measure how deep the hammock should be, then secure it by folding the edges over the mouth of the jar and tying a length of garden twine around the mesh. Fill with water to one-quarter of an inch from the bulb bottom. The roots will quickly find and reach the water. (SEE PHOTOS: 7, 8.)

6

Forced Bulb Care

Once the bulbs are planted, set them in a room where there is ample indirect light and a temperature around 60 degrees Fahrenheit. Add clean water as needed.

After blooming, keep the greens watered until the soil warms up enough to plant them in the spring garden. They are not likely to bloom again during the current season, but if they naturalize you will get to enjoy them in many a spring to come.

7

8

To force most bulbs indoors they need to be prechilled, with the exceptions of amaryllis and paperwhites. The best bet is to buy prechilled bulbs at the garden center, which should be available for sale in the fall. If you want to try your hand at prechilling the bulbs yourself, you need to set them in cold storage for 10 to 15 weeks at a temperature of around 35 to 45 degrees Fahrenheit. One way to chill bulbs is in the fridge inside a paper bag. Just be sure to keep the bag in a crisper drawer away from any other food. The idea is to trick the bulbs into starting their spring growth by faking winter. Note that each type of bulb will have a different number of weeks they require for chilling.

BULB	WEEKS OF CHILLING	WEEKS TO BLOOM
Hyacinth	1–12	2–3
Crocus	14–15	2–3
Muscari species (grape hyacinth)	14–15	2–3
Paperwhites	None	3–5
Amaryllis	None	Varies by species

JACK-O'-PLANTERNS

2

1

3

A PUMPKIN MAKES A WONDERFUL

natural container for fall plants. Add plants to a jack-o'-lantern and now you've got a sillier take on his scary cousin. This "jack-o'-plantern" may not spook trick-or-treaters on Halloween night, but the toothy grin and crazy hair will put a smile on the faces of those who come calling.

In cooler climates you can easily display a pumpkin planter for weeks before it begins to decompose. In warmer temperatures, carved pumpkins won't last long before they slump and mush. In that case start this project a week before the big day. After Halloween, remove the plants and add them to the garden (or another container) and toss the pumpkin into the compost.

MATERIALS

Pumpkin	Marker
Serrated knife	Container soil mix
Paring knife	Various grasses, cabbage, sedum,
Bowl (for reserved pumpkin seeds)	and ornamental kale

INSTRUCTIONS

Saw the top off a pumpkin with a serrated knife and clean up the edges with a paring knife. Remove the pumpkin guts and sort through to separate the seeds. Reserve the seeds for roasting (see "Roasted Rosemary Pumpkin Seeds") and toss the rest of the junk back into the pumpkin.

Use a marker to draw a face on the best side of the pumpkin and use the knives to carve out the holes. The serrated knife is best for sawing large areas while the paring knife is useful for smaller areas and finishing cuts. (SEE PHOTOS: 1, 2.)

Add container soil mix to the bottom of the pumpkin. Contrary to typical container planting instructions, pack the soil down at the bottom to create some firm areas where the plants can sit. These planters will not last long enough for the roots to struggle, plus they will have lots of moisture and organic matter from the pumpkin. Drainage holes are also not necessary. (SEE PHOTO: 3.)

Plant some "hair" with grasses or "hats" with cabbage. Fill soil around the roots of the plants and pack it in through the eyes and mouth. Leave space for sedum and ornamental kale as eyes and teeth. (SEE PHOTOS: 4, 5, 6, 7.)

Set your pumpkin out in the cool fall air and water. I generally water once when planted and then leave Jack to his own devices until the plants are transferred to the garden. (SEE PHOTO: 8.)

4

5

6

7

8

Preheat the oven to 375°F. Separate the pumpkin seeds from the membrane and rinse under cold water until they are no longer sticky. Pat dry with a towel and spread the seeds on baking sheets. For each cup of pumpkin seeds mix together

  2 tablespoons olive oil
  2 tablespoons finely chopped fresh rosemary
  1 teaspoon sugar
  sea salt and cracked pepper, to taste

Roast for 15 to 20 minutes, removing after 10 minutes to shake the pan and move the seeds around a bit. Remove from oven when they are golden brown. Allow them to cool before you start snacking.

ROCK SPIDER
SCULPTURES

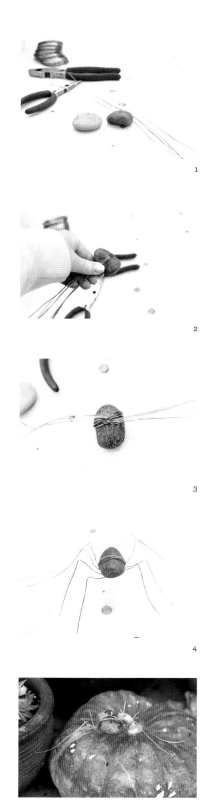

1

2

3

4

5

THESE AIRY LITTLE SCULPTURES

are simply made of stone and wire but they take on the feeling of movement by appearing to crawl, jump, hang, or sprint like the real thing. In my garden there are many of these little critters crawling around the pots and plants, frightening arachnophobes and mosquitoes alike.

MATERIALS

Decorative rocks approximately
   2" in diameter

16-gauge wire

Wire cutters

Needle-nose pliers

Hot glue gun (optional)

INSTRUCTIONS

Using the wire cutters, snip off four equal lengths of the wire 12 to 20 inches long. The longer the wire the longer the legs the spider will have. (SEE PHOTO: 1.)

Holding all four wires together, place a rock about one-third of the way down the length of wire, and wrap the long ends around the top of the rock to the back. (SEE PHOTO: 2.)

Fold the other set of wires to the back of the rock and twist the two sets of wires together with the needle-nose pliers to secure them around the rock. You may also use a dab of hot glue at this stage to secure the wire to the underside of the rock. (SEE PHOTO: 3.)

Flip the rock over and spread out the eight ends of wire. Using the pliers, create bends in the legs to create knees, which will allow the spider to stand on its own eight legs. You could also create a bend at the end of each leg to create feet. (SEE PHOTO: 4.)

Place spiders around the garden. Be careful they don't get away! (SEE PHOTO: 5.)

4

WINTER

PEOPLE DON'T USUALLY THINK ABOUT

gardening in the winter. The exception, of course, is those folks who live where winters are warm and the difference in seasons isn't all that dramatic. However, some of us lose the sun to months and months of rain clouds. Others have snowbanks taller than they can shovel snow onto. If you haven't seen the sun for weeks or your garden is under a mountain of snow, then my guess is you put the hobby on hold for a few months. To those of you, I emphatically say, "Don't underestimate the power of garden making in the winter!" The crisp air, the greenery, the smell of the outdoors: these things present all the benefits gardening can bring, even in cold winter months. Never fear—there is no need to bundle up and dig a hole in the snow. This chapter will cover the ways that you can get your green thumb in play even though the air is frigid.

When putting the garden to bed for the year, it's good practice to also make a bed for your garden workers. Take care of beneficial insects by providing them with a bug hotel as a winter shelter. Keeping them snug as bugs in a *hotel* can jump-start spring pest management by ensuring the good guys are safe and close by.

Indoor plants can be the ideal gardening outlet during inclement weather. Art pieces hung on the wall or miniature worlds hanging in a window beautify your home and allow you to get your garden therapy even though you're inside. Outdoors, you can clip evergreen branches and leaves to decorate for the holiday season. A festive wreath, a fireplace adorned with cedar, a hanging candle planter, and even gift tags can benefit from bringing out your bypass pruners. After the holidays are over, a Christmas tree can be turned into ornaments that will trim the family tree for years to come, each time bringing back many memories.

The boundary of a garden doesn't need to be limited to the space surrounding your home. Parks and forests are inspiring places to gather ideas for your personal oasis. Rivers and lakes encourage you to find ways to bring water to the home garden. Colorful trees can influence your own feature plantings, even if your landscape is on a smaller scale. The temperate rainforest that surrounds my urban home has been the muse for my woodland shade garden, full of the huckleberries, Oregon grapes, and maidenhair ferns found growing where I take the dog for his forest romps.

When you are roaming out in the natural world, take the time to gather a few treasures. Pinecones, branches, lichens, and moss are essential ingredients in many winter projects, and collecting them is a feel-good activity that will (snow) blow away those winter blues. Bring along a local nature guidebook and identify what you see. Perhaps in the woods near you the trees are covered with moss and lichens. How many plants can you identify? Is anything in bloom in the winter? Or fruiting? Can you see any animal tracks or hear any creatures chirping? A nature scavenger hunt is an energetic winter's-day project for children. Give them a list of items to collect and identify and bring the treasures home to make one of the projects in this chapter.

BUG HOTEL

1

2

3

A BUG HOTEL IS PART GARDEN ART

and part winter habitat for beneficial insects. These decorative displays of plant material are intended to provide shelter to overwintering insects, allowing them safety and comfort in your garden. Setting up different protected areas in your bug hotel will let the bugs find a room that suits them and prepare it as they wish. (To learn more about the types of insects that may move in, see "Meet the Neighbors.")

MATERIALS

One 4' × 6" piece of ¾" thick cedar or other rot-resistant wood, cut as follows:
Top: 5½" square
Bottom: 5½" square
Back panel: 5½" × 12"
Left panel: 4¾" × 12"
Right panel: 4¾" × 12"

Wood screws
Drill
Bamboo pieces, stems, twigs, seed heads, pinecones, wood shavings, lichens
Hanging hardware

INSTRUCTIONS

Cut a cedar board to the dimensions listed above using a table saw (or have them cut at your local hardware store if you don't have a saw). (SEE PHOTO: 1.)

Screw the box together by drilling pilot holes first as a guide, then using wood screws to secure the boards together. The side boards will screw into the side of the top and bottom boards, so lay out the pieces as they will be attached together. Hold one of the side pieces over an end piece where they are intended to attach and drill two pilot holes three-quarters of an inch from the edge. Screw the pieces together through the pilot holes. Add the other end piece and repeat the steps for making pilot holes and screwing the box together. Repeat steps for the other side of the box. (SEE PHOTOS: 2, 3.)

To attach the bottom of the box, set the bottom piece in place and drill four pilot holes, one on each side, and screw to secure.

Arrange the plant materials within the structure, packed tightly so everything will stay put, but with lots of available crevices for the inhabitants. Group like materials together and add some of the firmer items—such as twigs or bamboo—first. Fill in the empty spaces with different shapes and sizes of material, as if you were completing a puzzle. Nestle the materials into all the spaces until they are all firmly positioned, held in place by just the pressure of packing the box full. There will still be plenty of room for the bugs to move into the cracks, crevices, and holes. (SEE PHOTOS: 4, 5.)

Affix hanging hardware to the box and hang the bug hotel in an area of the garden that is near where you want beneficial insects next season. (SEE PHOTOS: 6, 7.)

4

5

6

7

Here are a few of the beneficial insects that you would be lucky to have as hotel guests.

Bees

Many garden bees are ground dwellers, so they won't have a need for a hotel room. They will dig a little hole in the soil for winter hibernation. You may see some groggy bumblebees when you are out digging in early spring if you wake them too early. Solitary bees, however, like to nest in hollow stems for the winter. Contrary to their title, they will often pack a number of bees in a stem before closing off the opening with some mud and then having a good snooze until spring. Bees are some of the garden's best pollinators and are essential for productive vegetable gardens and fruit trees.

Ladybugs

Ladybugs like to overwinter as large groups in between dry plant material. Twigs packed together give the ladybugs plenty of room to squeeze in and wait for warmer days. Ladybugs are not only the cutest insects out there, but they are powerhouses for keeping the garden clean of mites and aphids. Ladybugs will lay eggs on the underside of leaves, where there is certain to be plenty of food for the hatched larva to eat. Ladybug larva look like little orange and black alligators, and they hatch *hungry*. Those little critters will hoover aphids off your plants faster than you can say, "What the heck is that?!"

Beetles, Spiders, Lacewings, and Friends

Many other insects will have a variety of nesting needs. By providing different types of plant material in a bug hotel you will encourage all sorts of garden friends to lodge. How can you be sure that you are only providing shelter for beneficial insects? You can't. It's a tough world out there and at times bad bugs will move in. Some may even eat their neighbors. You can't control what happens in the bug hotel—just trust that if you provide enough space for the good guys, you can create balance in the garden. After all, if there were no bad guys, what would the good guys eat?

SHADOW BOX PLANTER

1

2

3

4

BEAUTY CAPTURED IN A PHOTOGRAPH

or painting remains unchanged year after year. What if the art continued to grow and transform before your eyes? In this project nature *is* the art, and it is fluid. A planter made from a shadow box frame makes for a marvelous small-space project where other houseplants take up too much valuable real estate.

There are some practical elements to consider when growing plants as an indoor vertical garden. Gravity will not allow for upright watering and sunlight needs are a bit different. It's best to consider a wall planter as ever-changing. The plants may grow full and lush, then outgrow the shadow box. They may protest the conditions and need to be replaced. The key is that you enjoy the changes and respond to the needs of the plants.

MATERIALS

Shadow box frame (see Note)

Thick plastic sheet (like a painter's drop cloth)

Staple gun

Scissors

Coconut coir sheet (often sold as hanging basket lining)

Indoor potting soil

Small-scale indoor plants

Fishing line

Decorative elements such as bracket fungi, pinecones, acorns, branches, and bark

Floral wire or other metal wire, 16-guage

NOTE: When choosing a shadow box frame, look for one made of plastic or another material that can withstand some watering. A frame material such as MDF (medium-density fiberboard), for instance, will not withstand water contact, so it is not the best choice.

INSTRUCTIONS

Remove the glass and matting from the shadow box frame so that you have a shallow box to plant in. (SEE PHOTOS: 1, 2.)

From a thick plastic sheet, cut a rectangle that is large enough to fit inside the shadow box and extend past the sides. Use a staple gun to secure the plastic to the frame, then fold the excess plastic back over the staples. (SEE PHOTOS: 3, 4.)

Cut a square of the coconut coir to fit inside the frame. Set it aside. (SEE PHOTO: 5.)

Fill the box with indoor potting soil and start planting! Remove each plant from the nursery pot and gently shake off some of the soil around the roots. When the roots are manageable enough to plant in the shadow box, dig them into the planter and cover the roots completely with soil. Even out the soil so that it is level throughout the box and reaches the height of the inside of the frame. (SEE PHOTO: 6.)

Cut openings in the coconut coir where the plants are; the coir will be used to hold the plants and soil in place. (SEE PHOTO: 7.)

Secure the coir by threading fishing line in a zigzag pattern over the coir and the front of the frame, and around the plants. With the staple gun, attach staples inside the frame; these can be used as places to attach the fishing line. (SEE PHOTOS: 8, 9.)

Use metal wire to attach the decorative elements like bracket fungi or pinecones to the display. Bend 16-gauge wire through a staple into the back of the bracket fungi to create a stake to insert it into the planter. (SEE PHOTOS: 10, 11, 12.)

To water the shadow box, set it on a tabletop and water lightly. Ensure that you are watering often enough that the soil doesn't dry out, but be careful not to overwater, since there are no drainage holes in the frame. Leave the freshly watered planter on the tabletop for six to twelve hours before hanging it back up on the wall, to make sure the water is fully absorbed. This project works wonderfully in a kitchen or bathroom where it is easy to water the planter on the countertop and hang it back up again in the same room. (SEE PHOTO: 13.)

5

6

7

8

9

10

11

12

13

Variegated foliage, vivid blooms, and heart-shaped leaves may be just the characteristics you are looking for in an indoor plant, but there are a few practical matters to discuss. Indoor climate, in many cases, is not optimal for plants. Without the sunlight, air flow, moisture, nor soil nutrients they would get in their natural environment, indoor plants have some challenges to overcome that their outdoor cousins don't have. Many houseplants are marketed as such because they are tolerant of these poor conditions. Tropical plants are often used indoors as they have large, broad leaves that absorb every ray of sunlight in a room, making them more forgiving of limited light.

The best you can do is choose the right plant for your space (garden center staff and plant tags are great help when choosing). Look for plants with care needs based on the light that you have in your desired location, the amount of space you have available, and the amount of care you are willing to put in. For the best results, keep plants watered, give them some fertilizer a few times a year, and change the soil each year. If you forget a few of these things, or for some reason your plant doesn't thrive, get a new one. Not every plant will do well and not every plant parent has the time to spend with their plants. I, personally, don't get too attached. If an indoor plant becomes an ongoing concern, I replace it with a more suitable variety. For other people, however, the act of nurturing difficult indoor plants is therapeutic. Your personality is the most important factor to gardening indoors or out, so choose what will make it the most pleasurable for you.

SAND ART TERRARIUMS

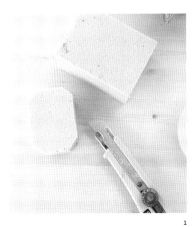

1

2

3

TERRARIUMS ARE NO LONGER JUST

seen as a revival of a retro 1970s craft. Modern versions have popped up in florist shops, furniture stores, and lifestyle shops. Attending a terrarium workshop is now a common activity for a bridal shower, and mini terrariums grace the tables of many a wedding. This newfound popularity is likely because terrariums are charming additions to home decor, along with being incredibly fun to make. The terrariums in this project revive another craft from an earlier era: sand art. Pouring layers of colored sand around the roots of a plant gives this project as gorgeous a display below the leaves as above.

MATERIALS

Florist foam

Knife

Glass vase

Miniature tropical plants for terrariums, in pots that will fit into the vase (cyclamen, *Hypoestes phyl-* *lostachya* 'Pink', and *Phyllitis scol-* *opendrium* used in this project)

Colored sand

Paintbrush

Cloth

INSTRUCTIONS

Use a sharp knife to cut the florist foam to a dimension that will fit into the bottom of the vase and is at a height that will allow for the plant you have chosen to be completely contained (that is, the potted plant should not be taller than the top of the vase when the pot is sitting on the foam). (SEE PHOTOS: 1, 2.)

Pour one color of sand around the foam to hold it in place. Layer in another color of sand, pouring until the vase is filled to the height of the florist foam. (SEE PHOTO: 3.)

Set your plant, in the pot, on the florist foam. (SEE PHOTO: 4.)

Pour layers of colored sand down the sides of the vase until the small pot is completely concealed. Use the end of a thin paintbrush to hold the leaves aside while you add the sand, and then use the brush to dust sand off the leaves. Use a cloth to wipe the sand dust from the sides of the vase, inside and out. (SEE PHOTO: 5.)

For a longer-lasting terrarium, give your plant lots of room to grow. If the plant's roots are crowded in the pot it was purchased in, pot it up into the largest container that still fits inside the vase.

Water with a dropper, turkey baster, or watering can with a thin spout that can direct the water to the soil just under the leaves. Excess water will flow into the highly absorbent florist foam. Trim back plants as flowers fade or leaves grow tall.

4

5

CONTRIBUTED BY JANIT CALVO,
AUTHOR OF *GARDENING IN MINIATURE* AND OWNER OF
TWO GREEN THUMBS MINIATURE GARDEN CENTER
(www.twogreenthumbs.com)

Creating a miniature garden in a terrarium can be fun and rewarding. The plants listed below will do well in open terrariums in bright, indirect light where the soil is left to dry out until it is damp between watering sessions. Water to moisten the soil only; the roots will rot if left to sit directly in water for too long.

Alpine water fern (*Blechnum penna-marina*) is a true miniature fern at only four inches tall. It prefers soil that is moist to damp, but not wet, despite its name.

Artillery plant (*Pilea glauca* 'Aquamarine') wears tiny leaves that perch on red stems and are the perfect scale. Pinch the tips to keep it bushy.

Baby's tears (*Soleirolia soleirolii*) has tiny, delicate leaves that form a dense mat along the ground. Control the direction of the plant's growth by pinching the foliage back carefully.

Miniature begonia (*Begonia prismatocarpa*) has pointy green leaves and yellow-orange flowers. Other smaller-leafed begonia varieties also work well as terrarium plants.

Creeping fig (*Ficus pumila*) is a fast growing but pretty evergreen vine with tiny, in-scale leaves.

Dwarf crisped fern (*Dryopteris affinis* 'Crispa Gracilis') is a beautiful dwarf fern with heavily serrated leaves that unfurl slowly.

Maidenhair vine (*Muehlenbeckia complexa*) has the tiniest red stems, with red-rimmed, round leaves. It is a bit fast growing and is best planted by itself.

Golden club moss (*Selaginella kraussiana* 'Aurea') wears a vivid green-gold color and resembles a miniature shrub.

Irish moss (*Sagina subulata*) is a great substitute for miniature grass. Tiny flowers in June will delight and enchant.

Miniature African violets (*Saintpaulia* species) and *Sinnigia* species (such as *Sinningia pusilla*) are some of the few miniature terrarium plants that flower. Plant these in their own pots to help protect the delicate roots and corral the water.

Needlepoint English ivy (*Hedera helix* 'Needlepoint') is tolerant and easy to grow; the leaves are deeply lobed but less than one inch long.

HANGING GLASS
TERRARIUM

THE FIRST TIME I SAW A HANGING

glass globe terrarium I fell in love. A garden so tiny yet complete, so contained yet accessible: how enchanting! I knew that I would have to create my own, and as soon as I did it became an obsession. Each glass, bowl, or vase I saw had the potential to surround a magical world filled with petite plants, found objects, and tiny toys. Through working with terrariums I've learned that a garden needn't be expansive to be artistic. A floating glass globe full of miniature leaves can be just as crafty and alluring as an outdoor garden.

Small areas require small plants, so look for miniature or dwarf cultivars. Purchasing a small plant from the garden center doesn't necessarily mean it will remain that size for long. Check plant tags to make sure that what you choose will be a good fit. Air plants are a great choice for terrarium living. Nestled into a seashell, these low-maintenance plants will thrive, without the need for soil.

MATERIALS

Hanging glass globe (see Resources)

Decorative rocks

Indoor potting soil

Miniature plant (*Pilea glauca* 'Aquamarine' shown here)

Dried moss and lichens

Other decorative elements (needle-felted owl shown here; see Resources)

Add some decorative rocks to the bottom of the glass globe for drainage. Create a base for the plant's roots to grow by layering potting soil on the rocks.

Remove the miniature plant from the nursery pot, retaining some of the soil around the roots. You may have to remove more soil so that it fits nicely in your glass globe. Use your hands to create a hole in the potting soil layer to plant the miniature plant. Fill in around the root ball with soil and press around the roots to hold the plant in place. (SEE PHOTO: 1.)

Top the soil layer with stones, moss, and lichens to completely cover it. Add any other decorative elements as you see fit. In the photo here, a tiny felted owl nests in the moss while a seashell houses an air plant. (SEE PHOTOS: 2, 3.)

1

HOW TO CARE FOR YOUR TERRARIUM

Terrariums have a unique microclimate from the world outside. Plants and soil enclosed in glass creates high humidity, so select plants that enjoy moisture and follow these instructions to manage watering and light requirements.

Watering
To care for your miniature plant, water the soil very lightly so that no standing water is left in the bottom. Use room temperature water—preferably rainwater, but if rainwater is not available use tap water that has been sitting out for twenty-four hours to allow the chlorine to evaporate.

Light
Place your terrarium near a window that gets indirect light for most of the day. Direct sunlight may be safe in the winter months, but in the summer move your plant to a window with bright, indirect light to prevent overheating the plants.

2

3

AIR PLANTS

Air plants (*Tillandsia* species) are epiphytes, meaning they do not need soil. They are found in southern North America, Central America, and South America latching onto larger plants with their roots and collecting water and nutrients through their leaves. Air plants make fun and low-maintenance houseplants, and they are wonderful options for soil-free terrariums. They can be displayed using just about any vessel, from a pretty ceramic bowl to a gnarled piece of wood. When planting air plants in seashells, find a fit by testing out a few different sizes. Snail shells, sea urchin shells, and other shells with a bowl or hole will work best.

To care for your air plant, thoroughly soak the plant and the shell one to three times per week (water more often in a hot, dry environment; less often in a cool, humid one). Air plants should be given enough light and air circulation to dry in no longer than four hours after watering. Be sure to empty the water from the shell as air plants will not survive in standing water.

EVERGREEN GIFT TAGS

BY ADDING EVERGREENS TO THE

garden, you are sure to have more than just a patch of dirt in the winter months. The evergreens in my garden provide year-long supplies for crafts and garden projects, like these gift tags. Snipping a leaf from right outside your door makes an easy decoration and it adds a little life to your holiday gifts.

MATERIALS

Evergreen clippings

Card stock

Craft punch or scissors

Jute twine

Small hole punch or sharp skewer

INSTRUCTIONS

Collect evergreen leaves from the garden or woods. Leaves that work well come from cedar, boxwood, pine, euonymus, holly, and hemlock. Some evergreens shed their leaves as soon as they dry out, so test a few kinds of leaves for their longevity indoors.

Use a craft punch to cut out the tag shape from the card stock. If you don't have a tag punch, then simply cut out a tag shape with scissors. (SEE PHOTO: 1.)

Using a small hole punch or a sharp skewer, make a hole in the top of the tag and two holes (side by side horizontally) in the center a half inch apart.

Thread both ends of a piece of jute twine through to the back of the tag from the two holes in the middle. Thread one end of the twine through the top hole from back to front.

Insert the evergreen leaf into the loop created by the jute twine and the two center holes.

Pull both ends of the twine to tighten and hold the leaf. Tie the two ends together around the top hole and your tag is ready to attach. (SEE PHOTOS: 2, 3.)

The closest thing to the Holy Grail in gardening is a four-season garden. I'm delighted to watch the progression of blooms or berries on the trees and shrubs: from holly to rhododendron to viburnum. The beauty of these trees is that they have their time to shine, then they step back into the chorus line for the remainder of the year. They create floating focus points that draw your eye around to a new area each week or month, creating an appreciation for that slice of the garden. Planting evergreens is the ideal way to continue interest in the garden when deciduous trees have shed their leaves and the perennials are asleep for the winter.

Evergreens can be broadleaf or coniferous. Broadleaf evergreens can be green or multicolored and variegated, often with white, yellow, and pink shades that add color through foliage as well as through flowers and berries. Coniferous evergreens are cone-bearing and generally have needle-shaped leaves ranging from yellow to green to blue. While they aren't as colorful as broadleaf evergreens, their shape, structure, and habit can all create stunning interest in the garden.

Evergreens are essential to four-season garden design, as their structure and form becomes an anchor in the garden. Dwarf evergreens can create the bones of a perennial bed: a basic structure around which to plant perennials and annuals. Larger varieties can be grown as hedges to replace a fence, create a backdrop, or hide an eyesore. Evergreens can become focal points as they soar to breathtaking heights or are pruned into a whimsical sculpture. Creeping selections can be used as ground covers where there is a large expanse of ground that would require less maintenance when covered, such as a steep slope. With the seemingly endless ways to add evergreens into a garden you should be able to find some to enhance your space no matter the season.

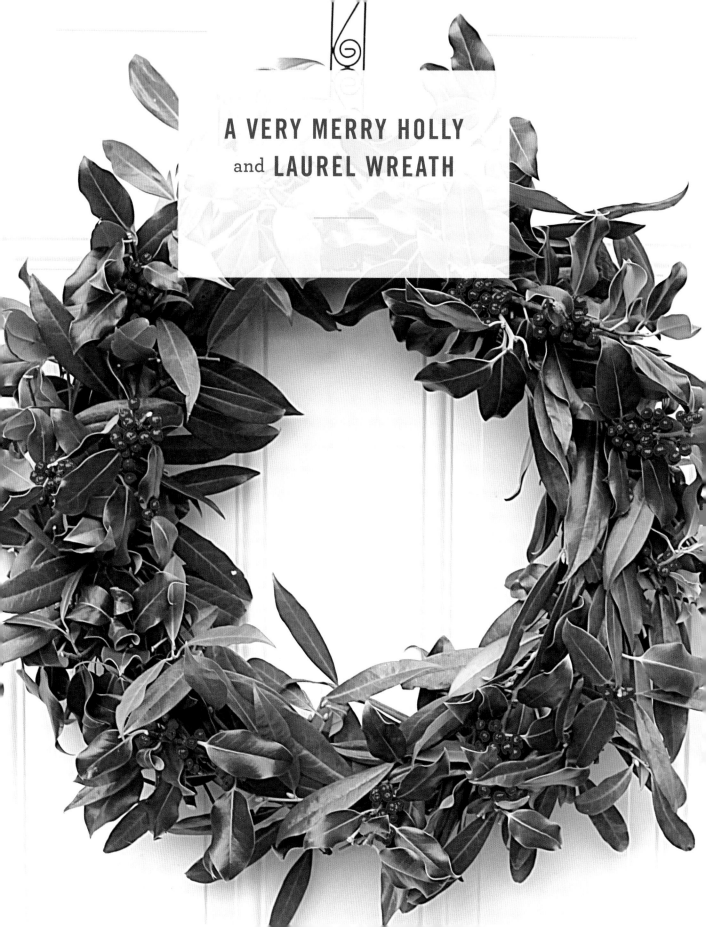

A VERY MERRY HOLLY
and LAUREL WREATH

NATURE PROVIDES SUCH FESTIVE

ornamentation in the winter. Those bright red berries on the holly tree aren't just for our enjoyment, though; they attract birds to a yummy cold-weather treat. Birds are an important part of holly tree reproduction: by coaxing our feathered friends to nibble on the berries (which technically are drupes, like olives, and not berries) they, ahem, disperse the seeds after digesting them. Now you know why there are little holly seedlings found all over the garden. If you don't want a thirty-foot tree in that spot thirty years from now, then you best grab a trowel and dig those suckers up.

Who would want a prickly plant like holly in their garden? The bees for one, who busily collect pollen in the spring, or the aforementioned birds who dine on the berries. If you have the space, you won't be disappointed by these festive trees full of branches just begging to decorate your home for the holidays.

To make a holly wreath, you follow the instructions as for the autumn harvest wreath on pages 108–111, using a grapevine form as your base. For this project, I advise you to use thick, rubber, rose-pruning gloves to protect your fingers (there are also smooth-leaf holly varieties, if you don't want to live dangerously). Have a look at the whole holly family and you will find variegated leaves and variations in leaf color. Berries can vary from red to black, white, orange, or yellow. Given that *Ilex* is a large genus of more than four hundred species of holly, you are sure to find something that will suit your preferences.

MATERIALS

Grapevine wreath	Holly branches
Laurel branches	Pruners
Twine	Rose-pruning gloves
Scissors	

1

2

3

4

5

Start your wreath by gathering a bunch of laurel branches. Add one holly branch with plenty of berries to the top of the bunch (you'll be happier if you're wearing gloves). Trim the ends of the stems to a uniform length, wind twine around the base of the bunch, and then around the grapevine wreath. Secure the bunch by tying the twine in a knot, but keep one end long. (SEE PHOTOS: 1, 2.)

Continue by making more bunches like the first one and winding them onto the grapevine wreath with twine. (SEE PHOTO: 3.)

When you come to the end of the wreath, tuck the last bunch under the tops of the leaves of the first bunch, then wrestle with the twine and the pointy leaves until you have that last bunch secured. Tie it in a few knots to ensure that everything stays in place. (SEE PHOTO: 4.)

Now have a quick look at the wreath. Are there any unruly bits? Use your pruners to shape the wreath and tame down some of the wild branches. Taking time to make these adjustments will make the most refined wreath. (SEE PHOTO: 5.)

Hang your wreath where you are sure to enjoy it most or to create a festive welcome to your guests. Evergreen wreaths displayed outdoors, away from direct sunlight and in cool weather, will last well for up to a few months with little maintenance required. Warm climates and indoor conditions will shorten the life of a fresh wreath, but keeping it away from heat sources and misting it with water occasionally can help to extend the fresh look. (SEE PHOTO: 6.)

You certainly don't want to harvest greens from your garden at the expense of your plants' beauty and health. A rule of thumb when pruning evergreens is to remove any part where you see one of the four *D*s: dead, dying, diseased, or damaged. This way the tree can focus on its health rather than fighting to save what has succumbed to a *D*. Once the evergreen's health has been taken care of you can prune for aesthetics. Whether you are pruning to improve the shape of your evergreen or to collect project materials, only make cuts that leave the tree looking natural. Stand back and take a nice long look at your tree. Follow the lines of the branches. Are there heavy areas that can be thinned out? Are there branches that cross into the middle of the tree to remove? Is there uneven growth that can be balanced through pruning?

When you choose what to prune, it's best to remove branches as close to the base as you can. Think of snipping off a branch that juts out to the side at a 90-degree angle rather than one that naturally flows off the larger branches. Prune back to a visible bud if you want the branch to regrow. Prune to the branch collar (the thicker part where it meets the trunk) if you want it gone forever. For best results trim only one or two days before you plan to make your projects.

A word of caution: never cut the top off a tree to cap its height. If a tree is too tall for the area it is planted in, you (or someone else) planted the wrong tree! Topping a tree only hurts the tree's health, making it susceptible to disease and further damage while it works hard to repair the trauma. The tree will send up new leader branches to replace what you cut; it will soon be tall again but its shape will be forever altered. Shrubs are another story. In many cases, they can be shaped and sheared regularly without long-term damage. It's wise to research the best practice for your particular tree or shrub, as there are many exceptions to the rules (except for topping trees—don't do it: it makes trees and people who love trees sad).

CEDAR GARLAND

FRESH GARDEN GREENS AREN'T

just for wreaths. An evergreen garland, or swag, can instantly cheer up a porch, banister, or fireplace. Garland can be made from a number of types of evergreen boughs. As a general rule, anything that you can use for outdoor wreaths can be used for outdoor garland. If you plan to bring your garland inside, the conditions are much drier and it will be difficult to water. I like cedar because it holds its leaves when dry and doesn't turn brown for a very long time. I also love the look of the draping cedar leaves as they flop over edges of a banister or fireplace. This garland has a casual form and makes a wonderful backdrop to display holiday decor: natural elements, such as oversized sugar pinecones, mixed with unexpected items, such as sparkly, vintage mason jars lit with a string of fairy lights, create an eclectic-natural look.

MATERIALS

Cedar branches

Pruning shears

Nylon rope (in black or green)

Green floral wire

Wire cutters

1

INSTRUCTIONS

Start by cutting the rope to the length of the garland that you want to create. Gather a nice handful of cedar and align the stems. Secure this first bunch to the top end of the rope with floral wire. Continue snipping cedar branches and securing bunches to the rope, overlapping and hiding the wire of the previous bunch. (SEE PHOTOS: 1, 2, 3, 4.)

When you get to the end of the garland, tie a few smaller cedar branches pointing the opposite direction of the other branches. Tie with floral wire to disguise the stems of the end branches.

2

3

4

Take caution if you decorate your fireplace with soon-to-be dry plant material (aka kindling). Do *not* build a fire if there is any danger of a spark at all. For this project, the gas fire is completely contained behind glass. Even still, the fireplace is kept on a low setting and is never left unattended. Safety first and beauty second.

PINECONE SPHERES

Make pinecone spheres by gluing the bases of many mini pinecones onto a Styrofoam ball with a hot glue gun. Be sure to dry the pinecones first so they are fully open.

HANGING CANDLE
PLANTER

1

2

HANGING BASKETS ARE NOT JUST

for fair weather months. Winter greenery staples like evergreen boughs can be snipped from your Christmas tree or collected from the garden. Left over wreath-making supplies will make this project even easier to put together, without skimping on style.

MATERIALS

Hanging basket

Soil

Plastic garden center pot

Bypass pruners

Evergreen boughs

Glass hurricane candle holder

Candle

INSTRUCTIONS

Fill your hanging basket halfway with dry soil. This needn't be the most nutritious compost you have on your property; any old soil will do. Its purpose is to merely act as a base to set your greenery in and it weighs the basket down just enough to keep the candle secure. (SEE PHOTO: 1.)

Set a plastic nursery pot upside down in the center of the planter and nestle it into the soil so that it holds securely. Ensure that it doesn't rise above the rim of the basket. Arrange cut evergreen branches around the outside of the basket, starting with your least decorative pieces and progressing to add the most ornamental last. (SEE PHOTO: 2.)

Add a glass hurricane and candle to the center, light, and it is ready to hang. (SEE PHOTO: 3.)

3

GREAT NATURAL CHOICES FOR OUTDOOR DECORATING

Spice up your outdoor garden by using cut evergreen boughs and decorative natural elements to decorate overwintering planters. Choose materials that are long-lasting and decorative, with berries, unique colors, and attractive shapes to add interest to the garden all winter long.

Greens

Magnolia
Eucalyptus
   (and seeded eucalyptus)
Cotoneaster
Pine
Hemlock
Fir
Spruce
Cedar
Oregonia
Boxwood
Viburnum
Holly
Laurel
Barberry
Mahonia species

Branches and Pods

Birch branches
Curly willow
Dogwood (red, yellow)
Dried badam nut pods
Dried lotus pods
Eucalyptus pods
Lunaria annua
Oriental poppy seed heads
Pinecones

TERRARIUM ORNAMENTS

ONE OF MY VERY FAVORITE THINGS

as a child was decorating the Christmas tree. Not because of the promise of presents or holiday cookies. No, I loved to unwrap the time capsule which was our ornament box. Packed full of homemade treasures made year after year, marking the crafts that we created as a family. There were salt dough stars, felt fruit, and golden-painted pinecones tucked amidst the glittery balls and strands of tinsel. Each year presented a new challenge of what to make for our tree.

These mini-terrarium tree ornaments were inspired by the winter my niece and nephews came to visit. To keep four busy children from getting into too much trouble we went on a scavenger hunt deep into the West Coast forest. We found animal tracks, mushrooms, lichens, and moss. We found leaves, pinecones, acorns, and rocks. The kids collected bags of treasures to take home, examine, and dissect. When it all was laid out we picked a few tiny treats to save in glass ornaments and mark the time we spent together.

1

2

MATERIALS

Clear glass Christmas ornaments
    (see Resources)
Decorative sand

Found treasures, such as stones,
    pinecones, moss, lichens, bark,
    and twigs
Tweezers

INSTRUCTIONS

The first step is to pull on your boots and go hunting in the garden or woods for fascinating things that are so tiny they have been previously unnoticed. It's a great exercise in appreciation of the small stuff that often gets overshadowed. (SEE PHOTO: 1.)

Add decorative sand to the bottom of a glass ornament. This will act as the base to hold items in place. In this mini wonderland, little lichen structures stand like people in the sand surrounded by a landscape of moss and bark. Use a pair of tweezers to get the right placement in the sand. (SEE PHOTO: 2.)

Hang mini terrariums with lights behind them to amplify the life within. Enjoy them for the season, then pack into an ornament box and store upright. Next year it may just take a little shake to settle the sand and set the scene again.

CHOOSING YOUR PLANTS

Tiny terrariums are best filled with organic materials that are no longer growing. While there are plants small enough to add to terrarium ornaments, like some air plants, it's not the best environment for them to thrive in. As adorable as they look through the glass, the basics of air, light, and water needs are challenged in a tiny space. Air flow is restricted by the small opening and cap. Light may be limited, or so intense that it heats up too much. All this and watering will take careful attention. This is not to say that making these ornaments with living plants cannot be done, but they will take a level of maintenance that I, personally, have no interest in. I much prefer these round display cases to have little scenes made of preserved nature like moss, lichens, pinecones, rocks, sand, seashells, bark, and more.

PINECONE MAGIC

Mini pinecones will open as they dry, so add a few when they are closed and people will wonder how the puffed-up cones ever got in there!

CHRISTMAS TREE ORNAMENTS

FOR AS MANY YEARS AS I CAN REMEMBER

I celebrated Christmas with a plastic tree. I never really thought too much about it. The ornaments are the stars of decorating for the season, right?

Wrong.

As I grew older, and fell in love with gardening, I just had to experience the rom-com-esque Christmas tree pilgrimage. Off to a tree farm in gum boots we went, sipping cider out of a paper cup and listening to carols played over a loudspeaker.

"Grab a saw and head out to the trees," they told us. We settled on a superb tree with the fullness, color, and needle retention that appealed most and hauled the thing up onto the roof of the car. The drive home was a sight: in every direction, trees were zipping down highways atop sedans packed with families, and I imagined all the people who would sip some eggnog later that day as they set up Christmas.

Our tree that first year was full of new memories, and offered a fresh evergreen scent that greeted me each time I passed by. The experience of choosing the tree out in the chilly air with pink noses and woolly mittens warmed me each time I added another present below.

When the time came to box up the ornaments and say goodbye to our tree, I had some trouble letting go. The needles had fallen and the branches were dry—but the trunk, thankfully, was just the right size for creating ornaments.

MATERIALS

Large branch or small tree trunk (see Note)	Drill
Table saw or handsaw	Wood-burning pen set (see Resources)
Sandpaper in both coarse (60 grit) and fine (150 grit)	String or ribbon to hang ornaments

NOTE: If you don't put up a fresh tree in your home but you still want to make this project, there are plenty of ways to get the wood. You could visit a tree farm and ask for off-cuts of large branches or too-long trunks. After the holidays you can walk down residential streets looking for discarded trees ready for recycling. Or find out where trees are composted in your area and collect one there.

If all else fails, you can go to a local garden center or tree lot after Christmas and ask for one they didn't sell.

INSTRUCTIONS

Once you have your tree or branch for this project, snip all the branches off as close to the trunk as possible. Let the trunk dry completely in a warm, dry place to avoid wood splitting. Cut the trunk into a few sections for faster drying.

1

Using a table saw or handsaw, cut the wood into quarter- or half-inch-thick disks. (SEE PHOTO: 1.)

Sand each slice of wood by hand with coarse-grit sandpaper first, then smooth the surface with a finer grit.

Drill holes through the top of each ornament so you can loop string or ribbon through.

2

Decorate your ornaments with paint, fabric, wood stain, or decoupage. In this project I choose to celebrate the natural look by using a wood-burning pen set. (SEE PHOTO: 2.)

To use the wood-burning tool, follow the manufacturer's instructions and practice on some pieces you are not overly attached to. Once you have the hang of it, you can draw your designs in pencil and trace with the burning pen, or just let some free-form shapes flow from your fingers. Snowflakes and stars are simple and festive, but try anything that is meaningful to you. Instruments, animals, initials, and words are all good choices, but there is nothing to say you can't draw monster trucks or cupcakes if that's what you're into. (SEE PHOTOS: 3, 4.)

3

4

ACKNOWLEDGMENTS

THIS BOOK WOULD NOT HAVE BEEN POSSIBLE WITHOUT THE MANY people who supported me along the way.

Zealand, thank you for all the Grandma Time that allowed me to do some garden making. Martha, the Oracle, I will never know how you can listen so long and hear everything, but I am endlessly grateful for your gift. Dr. Uwe Stender, you were determined to get this book made even though I was feeling too pregnant to imagine it. Thank you for the encouragement. Jennifer Urban-Brown and the team at Roost, you challenge me to be better: you found what I was trying to say all along. Thank you for bringing *Garden Made* to life. Janit, Genevieve, and Jacki, your generous contributions have greatly enriched my dabbling in your areas of expertise. Kristin, I so appreciate your wise input and guidance. Stacy Tornio, thank you for the nudge to write a book; it was you who planted the seed. Rob, Aymey, Hanaah, and Jaqke, I'm sorry I moved the birds but I'm glad they are OK, and the photos turned out great! I'm endlessly grateful to my models: Scarlett, Magnus, Mark, Leah, Evan, Matthew, and Benjamin.

Finally, to my family, who has been intimately involved in the whole process. Asher, my budding gardener, you clearly love the outdoors as much as I do. You were with me from the very beginning, and I thank you for coming along for the ride. Michael, you figured out how to make the crazy things I dreamt up, you Schneidered them together for me, and you've done it over and over again, patiently, while I took the photos, readjusted, nit-picked, and took more photos. Thank you for being my partner through it all.

RESOURCES

Garnish Garden with Soda-Can Herb Labels

CRAFT PUNCH: EK Success Paper Shapers 2-Inch X-Large Scallop Circle Nesting Punch (www.amazon.com)

Twig Garden Markers

WOOD-BURNING PEN KIT: Lee Valley Tools (www.leevalley.com/en/wood /page.aspx?cat=1,41115&p=31041)

Metal-Stamped Plant Tags

METAL STAMP KIT: 36 Piece ⅛" Letter Number Stamping Set by Pittsburgh (www.harborfreight.com/36-piece-18-in-steel-letternumber-stamping-set-60670.html)

STEEL BLOCK: Beadaholique Solid Metal Bench Block Wire Hardening and Wire Wrapping Tool (www.amazon.com)

Rustic Garden Sign and Mason Jar Tulip Vases

HIGH-GLOSS AEROSOL SEALER: Krylon Crystal Clear Acrylic (www.krylon.com /products/crystal-clear-acrylic)

Strawberries in the Sky

CHAIN BASKET HANGER: Tierra Garden 60-10050 Easy Swivel Rigid Chain for 14-Inch and 16-Inch Cone Planter, Black (www.amazon.com)

Flower Pounding

WASHING SODA: Arm & Hammer Super Washing Soda, available in grocery stores

ALUM: Jacquard Alum (www.amazon.com)

Modern Garden Planters

CONCRETE DYE: Cement Colorants, Lee Valley Tools (www.leevalley.com /en/garden/page.aspx?p=10342&cat=2,2180,33222,10342)

Mason Jar Solar Lanterns

FROSTED GLASS SPRAY PAINT: Rust-Oleum Specialty 11-oz. Frosted Glass Spray Paint, available at the Home Depot.

JUDY SEDBROOK, *The Night Shift*, Colorado State University Cooperative Extension, Denver County; www.colostate.edu/Depts /CoopExt/4DMG/Flowers/night.htm.

Citronella Candles

ALL CANDLE-MAKING SUPPLIES: Wicks and Wax (www.wicksandwax.com)

Felted Acorn Magnets

NEEDLE-FELTING TOOL: Clover Felting Needle Tool (www.amazon.com)

NEEDLE-FELTING MAT: Clover Felting Needle Mat (www.amazon.com)

WOOL ROVING: (www.amazon.com)

MAGNETS: Magnum Magnetics Corp ProMAG ½" Round Magnet (www.amazon.com)

Hanging Glass Terrariums

HANGING GLASS GLOBE: Hanging Glass Terrarium, CB2 (www.cb2.com /hanging-glass-terrarium/s479023)

FELTED OWL: Nuthatch Cache on Etsy (www.etsy.com/shop/alishaharms)

Evergreen Gift Tags

CRAFT PUNCH: Uchida LV-GCP74 Clever Lever Giga Craft Punch, Merchandise Tag (www.amazon.com)

A Very Merry Holly and Laurel Wreath

ADDITIONAL INFORMATION ON HOLLY LEAVES: www.telegraph.co.uk/earth /earthnews/9740540/Why-is-holly-prickly.html

Terrarium Ornaments

CLEAR GLASS CHRISTMAS ORNAMENTS: from Michaels (www.michaels.com)

Christmas Tree Ornaments

WOOD-BURNING PEN KIT: Lee Valley Tools (www.leevalley.com/en/wood /page.aspx?cat=1,41115&p=31041)

INDEX

mint, harvesting and using, 40
mosquito-repelling, 79
in seed paper, 13
holly trees, berries from, 150
Homemade Seed Paper, 12–17
hyacinth bulbs, 119

I

indoor plants
    and gardening during inclement
        weather, 128
    herbs, 9–10
    for shadow box planter, 135, 137
insects. *See also* bees
    beneficial, 128, 133
    winter habitat for, 130–32
Irish moss (*Sagina subulata*), 141

J

Jack O'Planterns, 120–23
June-bearing strawberries, 37

L

lacewings, 133
ladybugs, 133
lavender
    harvesting, 69–71
    mosquito-repelling varieties, 79
    types, 70
Lavender Sachets, 71
leaves
    harvesting for crafts and
        arrangements, 56
    pressing, 107
    Rhubarb Leaf birdbath, 41–43
lemon balm, 79
light, lighting. *See also* candles
    evergreen wreaths, 151
    for garnish gardens, 10
    Mason Jar Solar Lanterns, 72–75

for terrariums, 144
Trash-to-Treasure Solar Chande-
    lier, 80–83
living art, 49
Living Fountain, 57–59

M

magnets, refrigerator, 101–2
maidenhair vine (*Muehlenbeckia
    complexa*), 141
Mason Jar Forced Bulbs, 115–19
mason jars
    frosting, 73–74
    Mason Jar Solar Lanterns, 72–75
    tulip vases from, 27–30
Mason Jar Solar Lanterns, 72–75
metal, drilling holes in, 39–40
Metal-Stamped Plant Tags, 21–23
miniature African violets (*Saint-
    paulia* species) and *Sinnigia*
    species (*Sinningia pusilla*), 141
miniature begonia (*Begonia prisma-
    tocarpa*), 141
mint, planting and harvesting,
    39–40
Minty Sun Tea, 40
Modern Garden Planters, 66–68
molds, from rhubarb leaves, 42–43
moonflower (*Ipomoea alba*), 74
Moonlight Mojito, 83
Muscari (grape hyacinth) bulbs, 119

N

needlepoint English ivy (*Hedera helix
    'Needlepoint'*), 141
nesting materials, holder for, 31–33
night-blooming cereus (*Selenicereus
    species*), 75
night-flowering plants, 74–75
night-fragrant plants, 75

night gladiolus (*Gladiolus tristis*), 75
night phlox (*Zaluzianskya capensis*),
    75
night-scented stock (*Matthiola longi-
    petala*), 75
Nottingham catchfly (*Silene nutans*),
    75
nut caches, squirrels', 103

O

Ornamental Gourd Tea Lights,
    112–13
ornaments, Christmas
    Christmas Tree Ornaments,
        162–65
    Terrarium Ornaments, 159–61
outdoor eating areas, 81
overwintering plants, decorative
    coverings for, 158

P

paint
    choosing, guidelines, 81
    for mason jars, 29–30
Painted Mason Jar Tulip Vases,
    27–30
paper, handmade, 13
papermaking mold, 13–14
Paper Roses, 17
paperwhite bulbs, 119
Parsley Salad Dressing, 11
peat moss in soil mixes, 53
pebbles, forcing bulbs in, 118
peppermint, 79
A Picture Garden, 48–53
pinecones, miniature, 161
Pinecone Spheres, 155
pinks (*Dianthus plumarius*), 75
plant labels, 6, 10–11, 21–23, 93
planters

ABOUT THE AUTHOR

STEPHANIE ROSE IS THE CREATOR OF A POPULAR BLOG *Garden Therapy*, where you will find hundreds of DIY garden-related projects you can really dig into. Stephanie's creative take on garden making has been featured in *Woman's Day*, *Country Woman*, *Romantic Homes*, the *Huffington Post*, and *Apartment Therapy* among many more publications both in print and online.

Stephanie spends her time as a gardener, writer, and artist in Vancouver, BC, Canada, where she has turned her small urban yard into a "garden made" heaven, proving that size, truly, does not matter. She is passionate about organic gardening, natural healing, and art as part of life. Her mission is to bring the joys of garden therapy to everyone she meets, which serves her well in her volunteer work as a Master Gardener. Stephanie lives with her husband, son, and tiny dog, who provide her with inspiration and delight both in and out of the garden.

Visit Stephanie at *Garden Therapy* (http://gardentherapy.ca).